W9-AEG-692

LESBIAN QUOTATIONS

M. Seldin

2038

"LESBIAN QUOTATIONS"

compiled by
Rosemary Silva

Boston ♦ Alyson Publications, Inc.

This is a trade paperback original from Alyson Publications, Inc.,
40 Plympton Street, Boston, Massachusetts 02118.
Distributed in England by GMP Publishers,
P. O. Box 247, London N17 9QR, England.

Printed on acid-free paper.

First edition: November 1993

5 4 3 2 1

ISBN 1-55583-231-8

Library of Congress Cataloging-in-Publication Data

Lesbian quotations / [compiled] by Rosemary E. Silva. – 1st ed.
      p.   cm.
    Includes bibliographical references (p.).
    ISBN 1-55583-231-8 (pbk. : acid-free) : $9.95
    1. Lesbians–Quotations.   I. Silva, Rosemary E., 1962– .
PN6084.L45L47   1993
305.48'9664–dc20
                                          93-32373
                                             CIP

CONTENTS

For Himilce Novas

ACKNOWLEDGMENTS

I wish to thank the staff and the librarians, too numerous to name, of the New York Public Library for their generous assistance in my research. I owe special thanks to John Hammond, cofounder of the International Gay Information Center, for his recommendations and for directing me to the Rare Books and Manuscripts Division of the New York Public Library, which now houses the papers of his organization. I am grateful to Barbara Grier for her advice in locating material and for the superb bibliography, *The Lesbian in Literature: A Bibliography,* she compiled with Jan Watson and Robin Jordan. For their enormous devotion to readers and researchers, I wish to thank the staff of the Pat Parker and Vito Russo Center Library at the Lesbian and Gay Community Services Center in New York. I owe thanks as well to Rich Wandell, archivist of the National Museum and Archive of Lesbian and Gay History at the center, for stretching his hours for me and lugging box after box of archive material from storage. I am indebted to the Lesbian Herstory Archives, whose doors have just reopened, for reminding us that it is our responsibility to chronicle our history, that "memory is a people's gift to themselves." For carefully and enthusiastically guiding me through every step of this project and for making invaluable comments along the way, I wish to express my gratitude to my editor, Sasha Alyson.

Finally, friends and supporters deserve special acknowledgment. I owe many thanks to Virginia Day of Germantown Academy for opening the world of women writers to me and for that pivotal class discussion nearly two decades ago on women's oppression in Edith Wharton's *The Age of Innocence.* I will be forever indebted to Edwina Cruise, chair of the Department of Russian Language and Literature at Mount Holyoke College, for nurturing me during my college days and long after. I owe much to the uncommon women of Mout Holyoke, who helped shape my feminist sensibility. My heartfelt thanks go to Harry H. Derderian for a lifetime of friendship and humor, and to Rebecca Woolston for years of support and hours of research for this book at Princeton University's Firestone Library. My thanks also go to Pam Derderian, whose great integrity I have tried to emulate since childhood. Special thanks go to Alla, Boris, Aleksandra, and Daniel, whose Russian warmth and devotion have been a sustaining force. For their steadfast encouragement and support throughout the years, I wish to acknowledge my debt to my mother and my aunt Dorothy. Last but not least, I wish to express my gratitude to J.B., whose lively conversation over dinner in East Hampton about Anne MacKay's *The Wolf Girls at Vassar* and other gay gals inspired me to research this book.

—ROSEMARY SILVA

INTRODUCTION

> The Lesbian is one of the least known members of
> our culture. Less is known about her — and less
> accurately — than about the Newfoundland dog.
>
>> Sidney Abbott and Barbara Love,
>> *Sappho Was a Right-on Woman,* 1972

With little effort we can cite innumerable quotations of schol-
ars, poets, writers, actors, statesmen, and politicians. But the vast
majority of these quotations are attributable to men — white,
heterosexual men. Throughout time, men have been celebrated
and immortalized for their ideas, profound or baneful, on the
human condition. Furthermore, their pronouncements have been
collected and preserved in books of quotations, and many of
these quotations have been repeated so often that they are in-
scribed on the individual and collective consciousness. As Ben-
jamin Disraeli said, "The wisdom of the wise and the experience
of the ages are perpetuated by quotations." If we remember only
men's words, not women's, then we are merely perpetuating the
wisdom of wise *men* and *men's* experiences of the ages, and our
vision of life is tragically flawed. We are adhering to the denigrat-
ing myth that women have no history, no great triumphs of
genius, no pearls of wisdom worthy of remembrance.

Where is the inheritance of wisdom that women, lesbians
among them, have left us? Throughout the ages, women, no
matter their sexual orientation, have been barred from the very

experiences to which men have devoted countless treatises. Until rather recently, women in the United States did not have the right to vote, own houses or property, enroll in institutions of higher learning, enter male-dominated professions, earn fair wages, travel independently, go to war, or engage in politics. If, by some stroke of luck, women's voices have been heard above the uproar of men, rarely have our reflections been considered worthy of inclusion in the historical record. If, by another miraculous stroke of luck, women's reflections are preserved in the historical record, chances are they will not have made their way into a book of quotations, the highest honor that can be bestowed upon them. One need only try to summon to mind quotations by more than a handful of women to realize that most of women's words, women's reflections, are not on the tip of the collective tongue. A brief glance at popular books of quotations – *Bartlett's Familiar Quotations, The Penguin Dictionary of Quotations, The Dictionary of Quotable Definitions, Peter's Quotations,* and *The New Book of Unusual Quotations* – confirms this sobering realization.

Women, despite their oppression, have been prolific writers, particularly in the nineteenth and twentieth centuries. Alas, only a handful of books of quotations, appearing late in this century, have been devoted exclusively to women, among them *Feminist Quotations* (1979), *The Quotable Woman 1800–1981* (1982), and *The Beacon Book of Quotations by Women* (1992). These books represent a great leap forward in women's scholarship. They constitute a reconceptualization of history: they place women on center stage and write us into the script called humanity. How audible are lesbian voices in these collections? Unfortunately, they contain only a few quotations by, for, and about lesbians.

Thus this text arose from my perception of the almost total absence of lesbians from the pages of books of quotations. This book is an attempt to inscribe in memory the precious few recorded ideas of those women-loving women who, in some thirteenth-century corner tower, seventeenth-century garden, or eighteenth-century sitting room, blessed with an independent spirit, heatedly discussed women's plight and the pall of patriarchy, or sat alone, jotting by candlelight a passionate letter to a beloved or a few lines of verse devoted to Sapphic love. This book is an attempt to eternalize the words of the nineteenth-century lesbian who, biting her tongue, practiced self-censorship or wrote in code, assumed a male pen name, or changed the gender of fictional characters.

In collecting these quotations, my desire was to create a sacred repository for the words of those lesbians in the mid-twentieth century who, against all odds, came out of the closet to decry homophobia and crusade for lesbian and gay rights, and galvanized as a potent political force. These women excavated the works of their forerunners and began to piece together the historical, cultural, and literary fragments of the lesbian past, as witnessed by the substantial amount of lesbian research published in the post-Stonewall era. And finally, this book is an attempt to preserve in quotations the words of women-loving women who continue the fight against those bastions of heterosexism, homophobia, patriarchy, and religious fanaticism in American society, that perpetuate hatred and violence against lesbians and gay men, curb the discussion of homosexuality in the mainstream, and block the passage of legislation recognizing the rights of lesbians and gay men.

So that we may know more about the lesbian than the Newfoundland dog, I set out to collect quotations by, for, and about lesbians from a wide variety of sources. I have included homophobic comments in order to place observations by lesbians in a historical context, and to remind us how far we have come and how far we have yet to go in freeing ourselves from the bonds of oppression. I have arranged the quotations chronologically under each subheading. Only those quotations that add insight to a particular point under discussion are out of chronological order.

She stood silent for a minute, thinking; then she suddenly began again. "Then it really *has* happened, after all! And now, who am I? I *will* remember, if I can! I'm determined to do it!" But being determined didn't help her much, and all she could say, after a great deal of puzzling, was: "L, I *know* it begins with L."

Lewis Carroll, *Through the Looking Glass,* 1871, quoted in Judith Roof, *A Lure of Knowledge,* 1991

I like the letter L which contains its own shadow, makes and is made up of shadow, so that I cannot de-cipher the thing from its reflection.

Elizabeth Meese, in Karla Jay and Joanne Glasgow, eds., *Lesbian Texts and Contexts,* 1990

"L for Love," Beebo said, looking in space. "L for Laura." She turned and smiled at her, "L for Lust and L for the L of it. L for Lesbian, L for Let's — let's," she said...

Ann Bannon, Beebo to Laura, *I Am a Woman,* 1959

PART I

THE LESBIAN MOSAIC

TOWARD A DEFINITION OF LESBIAN

A lesbian is the rage of all women condensed to the point of explosion.

> Radicalesbians, "The Woman-Identified Woman,"
> May 1970, in *Come Out! Selections from the Radical Gay Liberation Newspaper,* 1970

If all Lesbians suddenly turned purple today, society would be surprised at the number of purple people in high places.

> Sidney Abbott and Barbara Love, *Sappho Was a Right-on Woman,* 1972

The Lesbian is every woman.

> Del Martin and Phyllis Lyon, *Lesbian/Woman,* 1972

A Lesbian is a woman whose primary erotic, psychological, emotional and social interest is in a member of her own sex, even though that interest may not be overtly expressed.

> Del Martin and Phyllis Lyon, *Lesbian/Woman,* 1972

All women are lesbians except those who don't know it naturally they are but don't know it yet I am a woman who is a lesbian because I am a woman...

> Jill Johnston, *Lesbian Nation,* 1973

What is woman? Panic, general alarm for an active defence. Frankly, it is a problem that the lesbians do not have ... Lesbians are not women.

> Monique Wittig and Sande Zeig, *Lesbian Peoples,* 1979

We do not become Lesbians by leaping into bed with another woman. We don't "become" Lesbians at all.

> Sally Gearhart and William Johnson, *Loving Women/Loving Men,* 1974

Lesbians are feminists, not homosexuals ... The crucial point really is that lesbians are women.

> Jill Johnston, in *Ms.,* June 1975

Lesbians are everywhere, even in the morgue. We die like anyone else.

> Rita Mae Brown, in the Foreword to Ginny Vida, ed., *Our Right to Love,* 1978

There are as many lesbians as left-handed women.

> Liz Diamond, *The Lesbian Primer,* 1979

We are everywhere.

> Message on signs held by gay and lesbian marchers in the Lesbian and Gay Pride March in New York City commemorating the tenth anniversary of Stonewall, 1979

If there's one thing that all lesbians have in common, it's the ability to say "no" to coercion.

> Julia Penelope, in *Common Lives, Lesbian Lives,* Autumn 1984

Potatoes are a lot like Lesbians. They're all the same and they're all different.

> Bode Noonan, *Red Beans and Rice,* 1986

Lesbians are first and foremost women.

> Laura Brown, 1986, quoted in Amy Appleby, ed., *Quentin Crisp's Book of Quotations,* 1989

The only thing true about all lesbians is they are all women.

> A woman from Washington State, quoted in Martha
> Barron Barrett, *Invisible Lives,* 1989

Every self-respecting, right-thinking, politically correct lesbian must know how to dance.

> Jay Thorne, in *Guide to Gracious Lesbian Living,*
> 1989

BY ANY OTHER NAME

Before *lesbian* came to be the generally accepted term to denote a female homosexual in the 1890s, the words *fricatrice* (1605), from the Latin *fricare,* meaning to rub, and *tribade* (1602), from the Greek verb for to rub, were occasionally used to denote a lesbian.

> Jane Mills, *WomanWords: A Vocabulary of Culture
> and Patriarchal Society,* 1989

During the 1920s and 1930s, Santa Fe and Taos were to American lesbians what Capri was to British homosexuals at the same time — a place away from the constraints of organized society, which discouraged homosexual unions ... In Broadway crowds at this time a woman who had switched her sexual preference was said to have "gone Santa Fe."

> Jeffrey Hogrefe, *O'Keeffe,* 1992

We didn't use the term *lesbian* so much then. We just said *gay gal.*

> Lisa Ben, on what lesbians called one another in
> the 1940s, quoted in Eric Marcus, ed., *Making
> History,* 1992

I am the rock that refused to be battered
I am the dyke in the matter, the other
I am the wall with the womanly swagger
I am the dragon, the dangerous dagger
I am the bulldyke, the bulldagger

> Judy Grahn, untitled poem, 1972, in Elly Bulkin and
> Joan Larkin, eds., *Lesbian Poetry,* 1981

...there are sub-sub-sub-divisions, between gay women, lesbians, lesbian-feminists, dykes, dyke-feminists, dyke-separatists, "old" dykes, butch dykes, bar dykes, and killer dykes. In New York, there were divisions between Political Lesbians and Real Lesbians and Nouveau Lesbians. Hera help a woman who is unaware of these fine political distinctions...

> Robin Morgan, "Lesbianism and Feminism: Syno-
> nyms or Contradictions?," *Going Too Far,* 1977

As women and as lesbians we have learned to reclaim names like dyke, bitch, manhater, golddigger, shrew, harpy, whore, cunt, amazon; (even) lesbian, even *woman* had first to be reclaimed from a place of squeamishness.

> Melanie Kaye, 1982, quoted in Amy Appleby, ed.,
> *Quentin Crisp's Book of Quotations,* 1989

In England, a Lesbian may be called a "wick"...

> Judy Grahn, *Another Mother Tongue,* 1984

A Dutch word for Lesbian is *lollepot,* a particular kind of pot. Lollepotten are Lesbians.

> Judy Grahn, *Another Mother Tongue,* 1984

...a Chinese word for Lesbian, referring to the Lesbian act of frigging, fucking with the fingers, translates as "stirring the bean curd."

> Judy Grahn, *Another Mother Tongue,* 1984

I always knew I was gay, but we didn't have such terminology. I don't suppose I heard the word "lesbian" until I was 50. Since I was always a university professor, I was always closeted and always socialized in an academic, heterosexual community. I never knew another lesbian except the woman who shared my life for 18 years.

> Monika Kehoe, in an interview in *Bridges,* December 1984/January 1985

Invert
Upside-down homosexual. There are many inverts south of the equator.

> Richard Summerbell, *ab•nor'mally Happy: A Gay Dictionary,* 1985

...I don't even think they have a word for lesbians. Women just don't come out of the closet. In Czechoslovakia they think that all lesbians are women who are so ugly they can't get a man.

> Martina Navratilova, *Martina,* 1985

In old Scotland the term was *dyke-loupers.* They had "louped" (jumped over) the "dyke" (the low wall that divided the fields) and gone over to the other side.

> Martha Barron Barrett, *Invisible Lives,* 1989

What *do* you call the person you live with? "Life partner" sounds legalistic and cumbersome. "Covivant" does have a delightful French ring to it, but seems more than slightly pretentious. "Living in bedlock without benefit of wedlock" is silly, but it does rhyme. Or how about "consort," "spouse equivalent" or "URAW," a Welfare Department term for a person living with an "unrelated adult woman"...

> Hayden Curry and Denis Clifford, *A Legal Guide for Lesbian and Gay Couples,* 1989

The very common "lover" sometimes implies an impermanence or predominant physicality which is not appropriate. "Partner" sounds financial, and "mate" conjures up images zoological.

> Sandy Rapp, *God's Country,* 1991

WRITERS AND ARTISTS ON LESBIANS AND LESBIANISM

If this little book should see the light of day after 100 years' entombment, I should like the readers to know that the author was a lover of her own sex and devoted the best years of her life in striving for the political equality ... of women.

> Laura de Force Gordon, in a note on the flyleaf of her book *The Great Geysers of California,* which was placed in a San Francisco time capsule in 1879. The time capsule was opened in 1979. Quoted in Dell Richards, *Lesbian Lists,* 1990

Teach us longing, the relentless embrace
Where pleasure weeps, faded among the flowers!
O languors of Lesbos! Charm of Mytilene!
Teach us the golden verse stifled only by death,
    With your harmonious breath,
        Inspire us, Sappho!

> Renée Vivien, "Invocation," 1909?, in *The Muse of the Violets,* trans. M. Porter and C. Kroger, 1977

These bewildering frightful beautifulnesses in this life – withal the same inherence which makes me someway Lesbian makes me the floor of the setting sun – strewn with overflowing gold and green vases of Fire and Turquoise – a sly and piercing annihilation-of-beauty, wonderful devastating to feel – oh, blighting breaking to feel – oh, deathly lovely to feel!

> Mary MacLane, *I, Mary MacLane,* 1917

And thus I see me in the subdivided cells:
a piece of a child.
a piece of a poet.
a piece of a Lesbian woman.
a piece of a writer.
a piece of a jester.
a piece of a savage.
a piece of something someway brave.

> Mary MacLane, *I, Mary MacLane,* 1917

To Romaine, to the unique and solitary artist
Every being in her portraits reveals its mystery;
Her vision is angelic – she, an angel with character!
Thanks to our friendship, to my first loves,
I relive my past with fire, then with light.

> Natalie Barney, of Romaine Brooks, one of her lovers, *Souvenirs indiscrets,* 1960

Through my own experience at Fawcett, it should be understood that a publisher (with the moral character of a nation in mind) cannot allow this theme [homosexuality] to be promoted as something to be admired and desired.

> Paula Christian, on the restrictions mainstream publishing houses place on editors with regard to homosexuality, in *The Ladder,* February 1961

Let us therefore respect these variants of the species who offer us their gifts: those singular beings who created works of genius instead of more dubious offspring, for it is known that the genius excels in production rather than reproduction. May those "blossoming peaks" of our race, whose only fruit are their works of art, console us for the multiplying mediocrity of humanity.

> Natalie Barney, *Traits et portraits,* 1963

A load of sticky jam with two adolescent girls embalmed in it.

> Violette Leduc, describing the main characters of her novel *Thérèse et Isabelle, Mad in Pursuit*, 1971

Lesbianism was "that awful thing" women did together, although at the time (and until very recently) I couldn't quite get my highly visual imagination to focus on precisely what "that awful thing" was. What I could do, though, was understand the words on book jackets. *The Well of Loneliness* cost thirty-five cents. The cover read, "Denounced, banned and applauded – the strange love story of a girl who stood midway between the sexes." The back cover started off with large blue letters asking, "Why can't I be normal?"

> Ingrid Bengis, on discovering *The Well of Loneliness* at age 10, *Combat in the Erogenous Zone*, 1972

It became the "Lesbian bible."

> Del Martin and Phyllis Lyon, on *The Well of Loneliness, Lesbian/Woman*, 1972

Gertrude Stein and Emily Dickinson
in your present lives
you are us
telling the truth
and living it too
at last

> Fran Winant, "Gertrude and Emily," in *We Are All Lesbians*, 1973

The fear of homosexuality is so great that it took courage to write *Mrs. Stevens*, to write a novel about a woman homosexual who is not a sex maniac, a drunkard, a drug-taker, or in any way repulsive; to portray a homosexual who is neither pitiable nor disgusting, without sentimentality; and to face the truth that such a life is rarely happy, a life where art must become the primary motivation, for love is never going to fulfill in the usual sense.

> May Sarton, *Journal of a Solitude,* 1973

There is no literature that is not based on the pervasive sexuality of its time; and as that which is male disappears (sinks slowly in the west) and as the originally all-female world reasserts itself by making love to itself, the primary gesture toward the making at last of a decent literature out of the experience of a decent world might simply be a woman like myself following a woman like Djuna Barnes, and all she might represent down a single street on a particular afternoon.

> Bertha Harris, in Phyllis Birkby, Bertha Harris, Jill Johnston, Esther Newton, and Jane O'Wyatt, eds., *Amazon Expedition,* 1973

The lesbian, without a literature, is without life. Sometimes pornographic, sometimes a mark of fear, sometimes a sentimental flourish, she ... floats in space ... without that attachment to earth where growth is composed.

> Bertha Harris, 1974, quoted in Adrienne Rich, "It Is the Lesbian in Us...," *On Lies, Secrets, and Silence,* 1979

There is no way of knowing how many such gentle novels, giving testimony to the power and sweetness of love between women, have been suppressed over the years, some of them not even committed to paper for the futility of the act.

> Jane Rule, on the novel *Patience and Sarah, Lesbian Images,* 1975

For me, the difficulty of being identified as a lesbian writer has not come in the forms one might expect: rejection by family, loss of job ... It came from other homosexuals who, living frightened

and self-protective lives, were threatened by the quiet but growing candor of our own.
> Jane Rule, *Lesbian Images,* 1975

It is the lesbian in us who is creative, for the dutiful daughter of
the fathers in us is only a hack.
> Adrienne Rich, "It Is the Lesbian in Us...," 1976, *On
> Lies, Secrets, and Silence,* 1979

I feel so good about who I am, about being a lesbian/feminist,
and I think this comes through in both the poems and in the way
I interact with people.
> Olga Broumas, quoted in *Christopher Street,* March
> 1977

To misappropriate Oscar Wilde's remark about the English and
fox-hunting: *lesbian literature is the pursuit of the inedible by the unspeakable.* It is also the pursuit of the unspeakable by the inedible; and
it is this particularly.
> Bertha Harris, in *Heresies,* Fall 1977

If just one lesbian, hidden in her hole somewhere in the deepest
provinces, finds out through me that one can be a lesbian and still
be happy, that there is neither shame, nor anguish, nor despair in
our condition, then I will have won my challenge.
> Elula Perrin, *Women Prefer Women,* 1979

Natalie is a pure daughter of Eve. Adam does not seem to have
been involved in her conception. Men — her father, cousins,
suitors, friends — are only very far-off worshipers who live on
another planet. Natalie loved only women, spontaneously, openly, at a time when hypocrisy and convention reigned all-power-
fully. Thus did she become the first liberated woman of her time.
> Jean Chalon, of Natalie Barney, *Portrait of a Seduc-
> tress,* 1979

I have burned many a book of lesbian fiction.

> Elly Bulkin, on the fate of lesbian works she read,
> in Bulkin, ed., *Lesbian Fiction,* 1981

She was far more than a priestess in a religion of Aphrodite, teacher to daughters of a dying gynarchy, salon-hostess to a bevy of active artists or just a lyre-playing Lesbian with lots of sexy friends. She wrote from such an integrated female place...

> Judy Grahn, of Sappho, *The Highest Apple,* 1985

So if you are a lesbian, be prepared. They'll take you seriously as an artist when you're dead. Then you can join the ranks of the angels like Stein, Cather, and Colette.

> Rita Mae Brown, *Starting from Scratch,* 1988

...lesbianism may be tolerated as an exotic activity but it remains a forbidden identity, and the artist stands to lose both privilege and authority if she is public about lesbian activity.

> Lynne Fernie, *Sight Specific,* 1988

The loneliest years of my life were those in which I couldn't accept myself as a lesbian. I didn't like myself, and I didn't like my life, and I couldn't write. When I came out, I began writing.

> Sarah Dreher, *Lesbian Stages,* 1988

The history of the lesbian movement, and the fiction that belongs to it, has been marked by a tense dialectic between openness and closedness, inclusion and exclusion, flexibility and rigidity.

> Bonnie Zimmerman, *The Safe Sea of Women,* 1990

Perhaps every lesbian has the secret hope that her book will dissolve homophobia, even in those straight people who, before they read the book, were unable to say the word *lesbian* without an overtone of disgust.

> Mary Meigs, in Karla Jay and Joanne Glasgow, eds., *Lesbian Texts and Contexts,* 1990

Writing the lesbian means writing someone who does not yet exist.

> Elizabeth Meese, in Karla Jay and Joanne Glasgow, eds., *Lesbian Texts and Contexts,* 1990

Our long-range goal is for any woman of any age, when she discovers her lesbianism, to have easy access to published materials that reinforce and validate this choice.

> Barbara Grier, on the goals of Naiad Press, quoted in *The Advocate,* March 10, 1992

FICTIONAL LESBIANS

Lois Lane is a lesbian.

> Jill Johnston, *Lesbian Nation,* 1973

Since 10% of the population is gay, then every tenth character is going to be also.

> Lanford Wilson, 1975, quoted in *The Advocate,* October 6, 1992

Most of the women in lesbian literature who own their own businesses make jewelry.

> Barbara Wilson, in Betsy Warland, ed., *InVersions,* 1991

MUSICIANS ON LESBIANS AND LESBIANISM

One of the nicest – whatever you want to call it – loves of my life was a woman.

> Joan Baez, in an interview with a Berkeley newspaper, 1972, quoted in Leigh W. Rutledge, *The Gay Decades,* 1992

...If a musician does a concert of woman-identified music, that can be a beautiful thing. It can create lots of energy, help women understand their lives better, create a bond among women. But that isn't enough if we're talking about really taking control of our lives. Because the rest of the world still exists and treats us like shit...

> Meg Christian, in an interview in *Lavender Woman,* February 1975

Lesbian musicians and their music introduced me to lesbian culture, old and new; helped me to understand lesbian oppression, and eventually gave me permission to admit I had fallen in love with a woman. I was astonished to discover that there were gay/lesbian relationships happening in every walk of life: nuns, housewives, movie stars, auto mechanics, athletes, and Congresspeople...

> Holly Near, quoted in the New York City *Gay and Lesbian Pride Guide,* 1982

This category should have been called "Best Lesbian Vocalist."

> Michelle Shocked, accepting an award for Folk Album of the Year at the New Music Awards in New York City, quoted in *Outlines,* February 1990

W hat happens is, a million dykes show up along with the normal dudes, and we always win audiences over ... if we were closeted, I don't think people would necessarily come in droves like they do, because we wouldn't be speaking to them so honestly.

> Gretchen Phillips of the group Two Nice Girls, on being openly lesbian, quoted in *Ms.*, November/ December 1991

I find that I like the energy of women in a concert. But they can be the most overbearing and disturbing fans, because they feel like they have a connection with you: "You're a sister. Gimme something."

> k.d. lang, quoted in *The Advocate*, January 12, 1993

ACTORS AND FILM CRITICS ON LESBIANS AND LESBIANISM

T he film lesbian is rarely happy.

> Joan Mellen, *Women and Their Sexuality in the New Film*, 1973

I just didn't wear any base.

> Tina Louise, on how she prepared for a lesbian part on TV, 1975, quoted in *The Advocate*, October 6, 1992

N ineteen seventy-four was the Year of the Gruesome Lesbian. NBC's made-for-TV movie, *Born Innocent,* showed two lesbians raping fourteen-year-old Linda Blair with a broom handle in a juvenile detention home, and a few weeks later, a *Policewoman* episode, "Flowers of Evil," had three lesbians murdering and robbing all the patients in a rest home which they owned. An actress who played one of the lesbian roles said she had been instructed to flatten her breasts, shorten her hair, lower her voice, and wear masculine clothing.

> Ginny Vida, in Vida, ed., *Our Right to Love,* 1978

According to this movie [*Personal Best*], lesbianism is just something you catch in the locker room, like athlete's foot.

> Rex Reed, on the film *Personal Best,* 1982, quoted in Amy Appleby, ed., *Quentin Crisp's Book of Quotations,* 1989

---

there has been a play on t.v.
a voyeuristic lesbian tale
the leading woman has a hard unvarnished
face   flat tits   dirty hands
her fate is some cruel joke   dreamt up
in script rooms over beer-guts and smoke

> Caroline Gilfillan, "lesbian play on t.v.," in Stephen Coote, ed., *The Penguin Book of Homosexual Verse,* 1983

I don't care how anyone identifies me as long as I can do my work.

> Lily Tomlin, on how she feels about being identified as a lesbian, 1984, quoted in *The Advocate,* November 5, 1991

The whole purpose of *Before Stonewall* is to show the emergence and development of the self-definition of gay people. And that's what the film is too. The film parallels that. It's not separate.

> Greta Schiller, quoted in *Bridges,* December 1984/ January 1985

There hasn't been a studio head I've worked for who hasn't come out and asked me if I'm a lesbian. I say, "Normally, this would be none of your business. However, I will answer you ...

It's possible. I'm not *practicing* at the moment, but I will not say it will never happen or hasn't happened in my past.

> Whoopi Goldberg, 1988, quoted in *The Advocate,*
> October 6, 1992

They called me up and said, "Here's the part. You're a dyke..." I said, "So far I like it." They said, "You run a discotheque and fall in love with Juliet Prowse and get strangled on York Avenue by Sal Mineo." I said, "I'll take it! Who could turn down a part like that?"

> Elaine Stritch, on what persuaded her to take a role
> in the offbeat 1965 film *Who Killed Teddy Bear,*
> 1991, quoted in *The Advocate,* October 6, 1992

We have no evidence of people running screaming from the theater because someone is playing a homosexual.

> Barry Diller, 1991, quoted in *The Advocate,* Octo-
> ber 6, 1992

There are probably all of three lesbian killers in the entire country, and they're all in *Basic Instinct.* America's 12 million lesbians are not pathetic creatures. We have wonderful, diverse lives. It's Hollywood's responsibility to show what's really going on in this country.

> Ellen Carton, on Hollywood's homophobic por-
> trayal of lesbians in *Basic Instinct* and other films,
> quoted in *Glamour,* May 1992

Nobody had it better than gay women in Hollywood. Mary Martin, Janet Gaynor, Jean Arthur, Kay Francis, Garbo, Dietrich – they were free to do whatever they wanted, and people didn't raise an eyebrow.

> Donald Spoto, quoted in *The Advocate,* January 12,
> 1993

ATHLETES AND FANS ON
LESBIANS AND LESBIANISM

And who are we to knock it if someone is gay? I think every man or woman has the right to choose how to live his or her own life ... There is such an injustice involved in Billie Jean's situation. She is the one whose personality, intelligence and charisma made women's tennis what it is today.

> Chris Evert Lloyd, quoted in World Tennis, July 1981

I've lost so many endorsements because of that. It's sad. It gets to the highest level, and then it's, "Oh, isn't she gay? Or hasn't she had relationships with women? Or isn't she living with a woman?" The president of a corporation may be my best friend, but he still won't take that chance because of the public ... I know also why sometimes I get boos on the tennis court from some people. They're booing my lifestyle, rather than me as a human being.

> Martina Navratilova, quoted in Ms., February 1988

Softball is the single greatest organizing force in lesbian society.

> Alix Dobkin, quoted in Yvonne Zipter, Diamonds Are a Dyke's Best Friend, 1988

Country dykes, city dykes, dykes with four-year degrees, dykes with no degrees, dykes who are feminists, dykes who aren't, dykes of different races and classes, dykes who have been athletes their whole lives, and dykes who are just discovering, or rediscovering after years, the values of athletic endeavors – there are softball players among all their ranks.

> Yvonne Zipter, Diamonds Are a Dyke's Best Friend, 1988

Lesbian jocks are a sexy and independent group. In fact, at the first Gay Games, women got so excited by the French dyke athletes that they auctioned off their track suits.

> JoAnn Loulan with Sherry Thomas, *The Lesbian Erotic Dance,* 1990

I can tell you what the L stands for in LPGA.

> Anonymous national sportswriter, quoted in *OutWeek,* June 4, 1991

There is no question that this is the gayest of sports — come to a women's golf tournament, and all you see are gay women everywhere. Yet there is this idea that nobody knows, nobody *should* know, and if anybody finds out, somehow the whole sport will just disintegrate.

> Anonymous professional golfer, quoted in *OutWeek,* June 4, 1991

There's a group of lesbian-bisexual players on the circuit, and they're the ones who get at the youngsters with their example.

> Margaret Court, quoted in *OutWeek,* June 4, 1991

The thing in sports that really pisses me off is that women athletes have to prove to the world that they are not lesbians. I was asked that question forever, even before I knew I was gay. They wouldn't ask a male that. The male athletes, the writers protect them. They don't want to shatter the myth: "My God, we can't have a gay football player." It's a macho sport. But the women they attack immediately.

> Martina Navratilova, quoted in *New York,* May 10, 1993

UNUSUAL LESBIANS

Mother Nature is a lesbian
> Message on a pin spotted in the Hamptons, 1992

Amy and Eve
> Slogan seen on a shirt in Greenwich Village, 1992

AFRICAN-AMERICAN LESBIANS

Black women are still in the position of having to "imagine," discover and verify Black lesbian literature because so little has been written from an avowedly lesbian perspective.
> Barbara Smith, in *Conditions: Two,* 1977

In San Francisco
with gay liberation
in D.C. with
the radical dykes
yes, I was there
& i'm still moving
> Pat Parker, "Movement in Black," 1977, in Elly Bulkin and Joan Larkin, eds., *Lesbian Poetry,* 1981

The black dyke, like every dyke in America, is everywhere...
> Cheryl Clarke, in Cherríe Moraga and Gloria Anzaldúa, eds., *This Bridge Called My Back,* 1981

Homophobia divides black people as political allies, it cuts off political growth, stifles revolution, and perpetuates patriarchal domination.
> Cheryl Clarke, in Barbara Smith, ed., *Home Girls,* 1983

As black lesbians who are on the threshold of the twenty-first century, we must repossess as much as we can of our woman-loving past to shore us up for the future. We can no longer allow our lesbianism to be defined for us by popular ideology, by the non-black lesbian ideal – though some of the non-black heroines may embody our values.

SDiane A. Bogus, in *Black Lace,* Spring 1991

As a lesbian of color, what I need is a revolution.

Barbara Smith, in answer to the question "What do gay men and lesbians want?, quoted in *Out,* May 1993

ASIAN AND PACIFIC ISLANDER LESBIANS

We must learn to see and be seen
to be so full of our pasts and our pride
that we can never be unseen
again

Chiyoko, "Untitled," in *Outlines,* February 1990

It is ironic, painful and powerfully joyous to feel so isolated and invisible ... in the straight Pacifica/Asian and white lesbian/gay movements, and yet know that we, as Pacifica and Asian lesbians and gays, are the *largest* lesbian/gay population in the world.

Judy Chen, in *Outlines,* February 1990

remembering the skinheads down on yonge
with their white skin sneers and swastikas

and nights when you think you're dying
it's the end of the world and you're going insane

and there are words for this:
jap, bitch, chink, dyke
> Tamai Kobayashi, "for renee," *All Names Spoken,*
> 1992

CHICANA AND LATINA LESBIANS

I am a Chicana lesbian from Northern New Mexico ... I have learned from my background that lesbians have lived together as recognized couples, or families, in my culture. The sexual aspect of their relationship, however, is often ignored; they are called "las tias, old maids, etc." so that the truth of their lives will not draw attention in the intensely religious atmosphere of their rural communities. There is much resistance to naming the "unspeakable."

> Jo Carrillo, in a November 1980 letter to the author,
> quoted in Elly Bulkin, in Bulkin, ed., *Lesbian Fic-*
> *tion,* 1981

The woman who defies her role as subservient to her husband, father, brother, or son by taking control of her own sexual destiny is purported to be a "traitor to her race" by contributing to the "genocide" of her people — whether or not she has children. In short, even if the defiant woman is *not* a lesbian, she is purported to be one; for, like the lesbian in the Chicano imagination, she is una *Malinchista.* Like the Malinche of Mexican history, she is corrupted by foreign influences which threaten to destroy her people.

> Cherríe Moraga, *Loving in the War Years,* 1983

It is a misunderstanding to say that gay and lesbian literature written by Latinas and Latinos is very small ... There is indeed a lack of critical work dealing with gays and lesbians of Latin American origin ... This problem is due to the immense biases that exist in the literary world towards both Latin American literature written in the United States, and homophobia.

Luz María Umpierre, in an interview in *Christopher Street,* October 14, 1991

D_{yk}-ana
Dyk-icana
what do i call myself
people want a name
a label a product

Natashia López, "Trying to Be Dyke and Chicana," in Carla Trujillo, ed., *Chicana Lesbians,* 1991

JEWISH LESBIANS

I had a chance to read a copy of *The Well of Loneliness* that had been translated into Polish before I was taken into the camps. I was a young girl at the time, around twelve or thirteen, and one of the ways I survived in the camp was by remembering that book. I wanted to live long enough to kiss a woman.

A Jewish woman, in a conversation at the Lesbian Herstory Archives, quoted by Joan Nestle, in the *Lesbian Herstory Archives Newsletter,* June 1992

As Jewish women and Jewish lesbians, we need to reclaim words like
pushy
loud
politico
power trippy

Melanie Kaye, in Evelyn Torton Beck, ed., *Nice Jewish Girls,* 1982

I want the issue of anti-Semitism to be incorporated into our overall struggle because there are lesbian/feminists among us who are threatened in this country not only as lesbians, but also as Jews.

> Irena Klepfisz, in Evelyn Torton Beck, ed., *Nice Jewish Girls*, 1982

The suppressed lesbian I had been carrying inside me since adolescence began to stretch her limbs, and her first full-fledged act was to fall in love with a Jewish woman.

> Adrienne Rich, "Split at the Root," 1982, *Blood, Bread, and Poetry*, 1986

Nothing had prepared us, and yet somehow all history conspired to bring us together: two Jewish women brimming with love for one another. So sweet was our delight, it seemed to infuse with meaning the centuries of suffering that had preceded us. "Those who sow in tears will reap in joy." We were the harvest; our love was the first fruit, the springing forth of life from the ashes of our people.

> Alice Bloch, *The Law of Return*, 1983

NATIVE AMERICAN LESBIANS

It is probably a little known fact to the gay community that prior to European arrival in this country, homosexual people were accepted by the Indian nations. They were often thought of as sacred.

> Barbara Cameron, in Ginny Vida, ed., *Our Right to Love*, 1978

The lesbian is to the American Indian what the Indian is to the Caucasian – invisible.

> Paula Gunn Allen, in Trudy Darty and Sandee Potter, eds., *Women-Identified Women,* 1984

dykes remind me of indians
like indians dykes
are supposed to die out
or forget
or drink all the time
or shatter

> Paula Gunn Allen, "Some Like Indians Endure," quoted in Judy Grahn, *Another Mother Tongue,* 1984

I feel like a minority within a minority in the gay comunity. You're in a subculture. In the Indian community you feel like you're in a sub-subculture. And the paths of the gay community and the Indian community don't even cross. I don't want that separation, I want all of it together.

> Leota Lone Dog, in an interview with Barbara Sang, in Barbara Sang, Joyce Warshow, and Adrienne J. Smith, eds., *Lesbians at Midlife,* 1991

DIFFERENTLY ABLED LESBIANS

Disabled lesbians face at least triple oppression – as disabled people, as women and as lesbians.

> Joanne Doucette, in *Resources for Feminist Research,* June 1989

It is not now or ever okay with disabled lesbians to be regarded as inferior. The truth is that we, the impossible disabled lesbians, are valuable; in fact, we are necessary for the strength, growth, and survival of *all* lesbian communities.

Edwina Franchild, in Jeffner Allen, ed., *Lesbian Philosophies and Cultures,* 1990

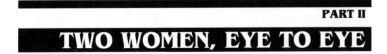

PART II

TWO WOMEN, EYE TO EYE

FRIENDSHIP

If Emma's bosom heav'd a pensive sigh,
The tear stood trembling in Elfrida's eye;
If pleasure gladden'd her Elfrida's heart,
Still faithful Emma shar'd the larger part.

> Anonymous, "Danebury: or, The Power of Friend-
> ship," 1777, quoted in Lillian Faderman, *Surpass-
> ing the Love of Men*, 1981

Davidean friendship, emulation warm,
Coy blossoms, perishing in courtly air,
Its vain parade, restraint, and irksome form,
Cold as the ice, tho' with the comets' glare.
By firmness won, by constancy secured,
Ye nobler pleasures, be ye long their meed...

> Anna Seward, of the Ladies of Llangollen, Sarah
> Ponsonby and Eleanor Butler, who eloped with
> each other in 1778. "Llangollen Vale," *Poetical
> Works*, 1810

To see her is a Picture—
To hear her is a Tune—
To know her an Intemperance
As innocent as June—
To know her not – Affliction—
To own her for a Friend
A warmth as near as if the Sun
Were shining in your Hand.

> Emily Dickinson, 1883, in *The Complete Poems of
> Emily Dickinson*, ed. Thomas H. Johnson, 1960

It was the age of great friendships: girls and even grown women carried the miniature of another woman about with them in a locket, bracelet or other ornament, would draw it out occasionally when in company, gaze fondly upon it, and press it to their lips; wrote long and loverlike letters to the beloved object, await her coming ardently, and wept storms of tears at her departure.

> Blanche Hardy, of girls and women in the late eighteenth century, *La Princesse de Lamballe,* 1909

This book bears no dedication. It ought to have been dedicated to G.F. ... and would have been, were there not a kind of impropriety in putting a personal inscription at the opening of a work where, precisely, I was trying to efface the personal. But even the longest dedication is too short and too commonplace to honor a friendship so uncommon.

> Marguerite Yourcenar, in a tribute to Grace Frick, her life companion, in the Afterword of *Memoirs of Hadrian,* 1954

A lesbian's best friend is an upside down cake.

> Jill Johnston, *Lesbian Nation,* 1973

It isn't just "good sex" we want, but good friendships, work, knowledge...   Nina Sabaroff, in Karla Jay and Allen Young, eds., *After You're Out,* 1975

...female-identified erotic love is not dichotomized from radical female friendship, but rather is one important expression/manifestation of friendship.

> Mary Daly, *Gyn/Ecology,* 1978

LOVE

The gods bless you

May you sleep then
on some tender
girl friend's breast

> Sappho (b. 612 B.C.?), in *Sappho: A New Transla-tion,* trans. Mary Barnard,1958

The roses will bloom when there's peace in the breast, and the prospect of living with my Fanny gladdens my heart: – You know not how I love her.

> Mary Wollstonecraft, in a letter dated June–August 1780 to Jane Arden, her first romantic friend, about her love for Fanny Blood. When Jane proved un-faithful, Mary sought the companionship of Fanny, who died prematurely in 1785. In *Collected Letters of Mary Wollstonecraft,* ed. Ralph M. Wardle,1979

She loved Ann better than any one in the world – to snatch her from the very jaws of destruction – she would have encountered a lion. To have this friend constantly with her; to make her mind easy with respect to her family, would it not be superlative bliss?

> Mary Wollstonecraft, of Mary's love for Ann, *Mary, a Fiction,* 1788

I love you with a love surpassing that of friendship. I go down on my knees to embrace you with all my heart.

> Madame de Staël, in a letter to Juliette Récamier soon after they met in 1798. The two lived together until Madame de Staël's death in 1817. Quoted in Maurice Levaillant, *The Passionate Exiles,* 1958

If thou wert not, what would the whole world be to me? No opinion, no human being has influence over me but thou. I am dead already, if thou dost not bid me rise up and live on and on with thee; I feel with certainty my life wakes up only when thou callest, and will perish if it cannot continue to grow in thee.

> Bettine von Arnim, in a letter to Caroline von Günderode, 1805–1806, in *Correspondence of Fräulein Günderode and Bettine von Arnim,* trans. M. Wesselhoeft, 1861

It is so true that a woman may be in love with a woman, and a man with a man. It is pleasant to be sure of it, because it is undoubtedly the same love that we shall feel when we are angels...

> Margaret Fuller, *Woman in the Nineteenth Century,* 1845, quoted in Carol McPhee and Ann Fitz-Gerald, comps., *Feminist Quotations,* 1979

Her brow is fit for thrones
But I have not a crest.
Her heart is fit for *home–*
I – a Sparrow – build there
Sweet of twigs and twine
My perennial nest.

> Emily Dickinson, 1859, in *The Complete Poems of Emily Dickinson,* ed. Thomas H. Johnson,1960

Golden head by golden head,
Like two pigeons in one nest
Folded in each other's wings,
They lay down in their curtained bed:
Like two blossoms on one stem,
Like two flakes of new-fallen snow,

Like two wands of ivory
Tipped with gold for awful kings.

> Christina Rossetti, of Laura and Lizzie. "Goblin
> Market," 1861, in Cora Kaplan, ed., *Salt and Bitter
> and Good,* 1975

A̲ll distance may this hower destroy,
Confirme your love, begin your joy!
O how much kindnes does afford
That pleasant, & that mighty word!

If you these termes do disapprove,
Ye cannot, or ye will not love.
But if ye like these lovely bands,
With them join hearts, & lips, & hands.

> Katherine Philips, "To Rosania and Lucasia, Articles
> of Friendship," 1861?, in *The Collected Works of
> Katherine Philips,* Vol. 1, ed. Patrick Thomas, 1990

A̲h, how I love you, it paralyzes me – It makes me heavy with
emotion ... I tremble at the thought of you – all my whole being
leans out to you ... I dare not think of your arms.

> Evangeline Marrs Simpson Whipple to Rose Eliza-
> beth Cleveland, President Grover Cleveland's sis-
> ter, 1890. In a letter to Evangeline, Rose writes:
> "How much kissing can Cleopatra stand?" In 1910
> the two women went to Italy, where they stayed
> together until Rose's death in 1918. Evangeline,
> who died in 1930, was buried near Rose. Quoted
> in Lillian Faderman, *Odd Girls and Twilight Lovers,*
> 1991

I̲ love her with the seasons, with the winds,
As the stars worship, as anemones
Shudder in secret for the sun, as bees
Buzz round an open flower: in all kinds

My love is perfect; and in each she finds
Herself the goal

> Michael Field (pseudonym of Katherine Bradley
> and Edith Cooper), "Constancy," *Underneath the
> Bough,* 1898

Without a sound, in the silent ardor of deep, blissful joy,
we lay in each other's arms.
And the breath of our beating pulses was just enough to let
us speak the beloved name—
"Lenore."
"Yvette."

> Elizabeth Dauthendey, who later describes lesbian-
> ism as a solution "for the famishing woman ...
> whose ... new self cannot tolerate the love of man
> as he is." *Of the New Woman and Her Love: A Book
> for Mature Minds,* 1900

Life has prepared a soft bed for you
If gentle woman's love is yours.
You will not be robbed of it in later years,
For it rests not merely on beauty and assets.
However warm and abundant you are, however selfless,
In the same measure you will be paid back.

> Marie von Najmajer, "Hymn to the Daughter of the
> Twentieth Century," 1900, quoted in the Introduc-
> tion to Lillian Faderman and Brigitte Eriksson, *Les-
> bians in Germany 1890's –1920's,* 1990

Are there many things in this cool-hearted world so utterly
exquisite as the pure love of one woman for another?

> Mary MacLane, *The Story of Mary MacLane, by
> Herself,* 1902

There is love
of woman unto woman, in its fibre
Stronger than knits a mother to her child.
There is no lack of it, and no defect;
It looks nor up nor down,
But loves from plentitude to plentitude.

> Michael Field (pseudonym of Katherine Bradley
> and Edith Cooper), *The Tragedy of Pardon, and
> Diane,* 1911

The room is filled with the strange scent
Of wistaria blossoms.
They sway in the moon's radiance
And tap against the wall.
But the cup of my heart is still,
And cold, and empty.

When you come, it brims
Red and trembling with blood

> Amy Lowell, of Ada Russell, "Absence," *Sword
> Blades and Poppy Seed,* 1914

But I look at you, heart of silver,
White heart-flame of polished silver,
Burning beneath the blue steeples of the larkspur,
And I long to kneel instantly at your feet

> Amy Lowell, of Ada Russell, "Madonna of the Eve-
> ning Flowers," 1919, in *The Complete Poetical
> Works of Amy Lowell,* 1955

There are so many ways to love
And each way has its own delight—
Then be content to come to me
Only as spray the beating sea
Drives inland through the night.

> Sara Teasdale, "Spray," *Flame and Shadow,* 1920

I love my love with a dress and a hat
I love my love and not with this or with that
I love my love with a y because she is my bride
I love her with a d because she is my love beside

> Gertrude Stein, "Before the Flowers of Friendship
> Faded Friendship Faded," 1931, in Stephen Coote,
> ed., *The Penguin Book of Homosexual Verse*, 1983

Oh! I want to put my arms around you, I ache to hold you close. Your ring is a great comfort. I look at it & think she does love me or I wouldn't be wearing it!

> Eleanor Roosevelt, in a letter to Lorena Hickok,
> March 7, 1933, quoted in Doris Faber, *The Life of
> Lorena Hickok: E.R.'s Friend*, 1980

A so-called Lesbian alliance can be of rarefied purity, and those who do not believe it are merely judging in ignorance of the facts.

> Elisabeth Craigin, *Either Is Love*, 1937

Between women love is contemplative; caresses are intended less to gain possession of the other than gradually to re-create the self through her; separateness is abolished, there is no struggle, no victory, no defeat; in exact reciprocity each is at once subject and object, sovereign and slave; duality becomes mutuality.

> Simone de Beauvoir, *The Second Sex*, 1953

"...A lot of strange things have been done in the name of love. In the search for love. And for the love of women. Crazy, silly, unreasonable things..."

> Ann Bannon, Beebo to Beth, *Journey to a Woman*,
> 1960

"Love me, Evelyn."
"I do."

> Jane Rule, Ann to Evelyn, *Desert of the Heart,* 1964

"The only real love I have ever felt
was for children and other women.
Everything else was lust, pity,
self-hatred, pity, lust."
This is a woman's confession.

> Adrienne Rich, "The Phenomenology of Anger,"
> *Diving into the Wreck,* 1973

My love is water.
I swim in her arms,
Struggling toward what new land?
Visions of it catch at my mind
As, buffeted, sustained,
I change, I change.

> Barbara Deming, untitled, *We Cannot Live without
> Our Lives,* 1974

Love between women is seen as a paradigm of love between
equals, and that is perhaps its greatest attraction.

> Elizabeth Janeway, *Between Myth and Morning,*
> 1974

Being a woman loving women ... the lines blur. With great
beauty though, like undulating lines of sun on the waves, in the
middle of the ocean, half-way between one continent and the
next, the lines of definition barely existing, at least always moving, never holding still, between being a woman loving yourself
and being a woman loving women. Same breasts. Same warm
skin. Same softness, and particularly female sense of life and joy,
such laughter and nurturing possible.

> Irene Yarrow, "Woman Becoming," in Gina Covina
> and Laurel Galana, eds., *The Lesbian Reader,* 1975

Y ou are m/y glory of cyprine m/y tawny lilac purple one, you pursue m/e throughout m/y tunnels, your wind bursts in, you blow in m/y ears, you bellow, your cheeks are flushed, you are m/yself you are m/yself (aid m/e Sappho) you are m/yself...
> Monique Wittig, *The Lesbian Body,* 1975

...t wo women, eye to eye
measuring each other's spirit, each other's
limitless desire,
> a whole new poetry beginning here.
> Adrienne Rich, "Transcendental Etude," 1977, *The Dream of a Common Language,* 1978

I magine my surprise,
Now that I have found you,
And I ache all over wanting to know your every dream.
Imagine my surprise
To find that I love you
Feeling warm all over knowing that you've been alive.
> Holly Near, from the song "Imagine My Surprise," on the album *Imagine My Surprise,* 1978

W omen have always loved women.
> Elaine Marks, in George Stambolian and Elaine Marks, eds., *Homosexualities and French Literature,* 1979

F or the love between women is nothing like the love of men. I love you for yourself and not for myself. I desire from you only your smiling lips and the brightness of your gaze.
> Renée Vivien, "Bona Dea," in *The Woman of the Wolf and Other Stories,* 1983

F rom Vicky, Annie felt no ending, but an opening, a doorway to a path ... She pictured Vicky and herself hand in hand on a path in the mountains, barefoot, the grasses and clover tickling their ankles. They climbed higher and higher. At each new elevation they became giddier from the purity of the air and their feelings ... For a love like this what would Annie not do!

> Lee Lynch, of Annie and Victoria, *Toothpick House*, 1983

The love expressed between women is particular and powerful, because we have had to love in order to live; love has been our survival.

> Audre Lorde, in Mari Evans, ed., *Black Women Writers*, 1983

I have seen lesbian plums which cling to each other
in the tightest of monogamous love
and I have watched lesbian pumpkins
declare the whole patch their playground.

> Martha Courtot, 1984, quoted in Amy Appleby, ed., *Quentin Crisp's Book of Quotations*, 1989

And I fell in love with a woman so tall that
when I looked at her eyes I had to go star-gazing.

> Suniti Namjoshi, "From the Travels of Gulliver," in Carl Morse and Joan Larkin, eds., *Gay and Lesbian Poetry in Our Time*, 1988

PASSION

In the intimate dark there's never an ear,
Though the tulips stand on tiptoe to hear.
So give; ripe fruit must shrivel or fall.
As you are mine, Sweetheart, give all!

> Amy Lowell, "Hora Stellatrix," *A Dome of Many-Coloured Glass*, 1912

Lifting belly is proud.
Lifting belly my queen.
Lifting belly happy.
Lifting belly see.

> Gertrude Stein, "Lifting Belly," 1915–1917, in *The Yale Gertrude Stein*, ed. Richard Kostelanetz, 1980

I break wild roses, scatter them over her.
The thorns between us sting like love's pain.
Her flesh, bitter and salt to my tongue,
I taste with endless kisses and taste again.

> Elsa Gidlow, "For the Goddess Too Well Known," 1919, in Elly Bulkin and Joan Larkin, eds., *Lesbian Poetry*, 1981

Well, the whole summer she was mine – a mad and irresponsible summer of moonlight nights, and infinite escapades, and passionate letters, and music, and poetry. Things were not tragic for us then, because although we cared passionately we didn't care deeply – not like now, though it was deepening all the time...

> Vita Sackville-West, of a summer spent with Violet Trefusis, in a diary entry for September 29, 1920. Quoted in Nigel Nicolson, *Portrait of a Marriage*, 1973

I am being led I am being led I am being gently led to bed.
I am being led I am being led I am being gently led.

> Gertrude Stein, "Didn't Nelly and Lilly Love You," 1922, in *As Fine as Melanctha (1914–1930)*, ed. Carl Van Vechten, 1954

Dined with Virginia at Richmond. She is as delicious as ever.

> Vita Sackville-West, of Virginia Woolf, in a diary entry for February 22, 1923. Quoted in Nigel Nicolson, *Portrait of a Marriage*, 1973

Then came the most exquisite moment of her life passing a stone urn with flowers in it. Sally stopped; picked a flower; kissed her on the lips. The whole world might have turned upside down! The others had disappeared; there she was alone with Sally. And she felt that she had been given a present, wrapped up, and told just to keep it, not to look at it – a diamond, something infinitely precious...

> Virgina Woolf, describing Clarissa Dalloway's sentiments about Sally, *Mrs. Dalloway,* 1925

No, I am in no muddles [love affairs] ... Dorothy I have not seen. Louise, no muddles (either Genoux or Loraine), Vera, no muddles. Lady Hillingdon, no muddles; don't know her; don't want to. Violet [Trefusis], no muddles; don't even know where she is; don't want to get into touch, thank you. Virginia [Woolf] – not a muddle exactly; she is a busy and sensible woman. But she does love me, and I did sleep with her at Rodmell. That does not constitute a muddle though.

> Vita Sackville-West, in a letter dated June 28, 1926, to her husband Harold Nicolson about her affair with Virginia Woolf. In *Vita and Harold,* ed. Nigel Nicolson, 1992

In living amorously together, two women may eventually discover that their mutual attraction is not basically sensual ... What woman would not blush to seek out her *amie* only for sensual pleasure? In no way is it passion that fosters the devotion of two women, but rather a feeling of kinship.

> Sidonie Gabrielle Colette, *Ces plaisirs,* 1932

Adventure is making the distant approach nearer but romance is having what is where it is which is not where you are stay where it is.

> Gertrude Stein, "An American and France," *What Are Masterpieces,* 1940

There is nothing mysterious or magical about Lesbian lovemaking ... The mystery and the magic come from the person with whom you are making love.

> Del Martin and Phyllis Lyon, *Lesbian/Woman,* 1972

What's it like for two women to make love?
   Pretty much as you would expect.

> Elana Nachman/Dykewomon, *Riverfinger Women,*
> 1974

I imagine, starved to death, that I am making love to her in my first memory. I am in some summerhouse, in some country with a season of heat no other place in the world can match. It could be Alabama; it could be the isle of Capri and I a wealthy, pre-war lesbian ... There is nothing inside the summerhouse but the two of us and that broken shard of teacup where a sleeping garter snake lies curled.

> Bertha Harris, *Lover,* 1976

We cross the street, kissing
against the light, singing, *This
is the woman I woke from sleep, the woman that woke
me sleeping.*

> Olga Broumas, "Sleeping Beauty," *Beginning with
> O,* 1977

Whatever happens with us, your body
will haunt mine − tender, delicate
your lovemaking, like the half-curled frond
of the fiddlehead fern in forests
just washed by sun. Your traveled, generous thighs
between which my whole face has come and come−

> Adrienne Rich, "The Floating Poem, Unnumbered,"
> *The Dream of a Common Language,* 1978

Of course a lesbian is more than her body, more than her flesh, but lesbianism partakes of the body, partakes of the flesh. That carnality distinguishes it from gestures of political sympathy with homosexuals and from affectionate friendships in which women enjoy each other, support each other, and commingle a sense of identity and well-being. Lesbianism represents a commitment of skin, blood, breast, and bone.

> Catharine R. Stimpson, in Elizabeth Abel, ed., *Writing and Sexual Difference,* 1982

After the supper dishes, let us start
where we left off, my knees between your knees,
half in the window seat. O let me, please,
hands in your hair, drink in your mouth. Sweetheart,
your body is a text I need the art
to be constructed by...

> Marilyn Hacker, "Future Conditional," *Love, Death and the Changing of the Seasons,* 1986

Lesbian lovemaking, contrary to what Reuben thinks, does not equal zero. It equals, among other things, orgasm.

> Dolores Klaich, in response to David Reuben's comment in *Everything You Always Wanted to Know about Sex* that "just as one penis plus one penis equals nothing, one vagina plus another vagina still equals zero." *Woman Plus Woman,* 1989

Once, I actually heard two women doing it over the phone. It was very hot until one of them asked for the clitoris size of the other. I had never really thought about dyke size queens, and when I did I thought it would be a breast fetish. I had to hang up so I didn't ruin their evening with sarcasm.

> Liz Tracey, on her experiences with lesbian sex lines, in *OutWeek,* quoted in *Outlines,* February 1990

A lot of people in England still find it difficult to believe lesbians *do* anything. Except perhaps knit together.

> Dame Maggie Smith, 1990, quoted in *The Advocate*, October 6, 1992

W hen I say things like – "I would like to deconstruct
your prose and perhaps do other nifty, radical, abstract
things"–
> it does something.

> E.D. Hernández, "A Love Poem 1989," in Carla
> Trujillo, ed., *Chicana Lesbians,* 1991

A ll of my sexual experiences when I was young were with girls.
I mean, we didn't have those sleep-over parties for nothing.

> Madonna, 1991, quoted in *The Advocate,* October
> 6, 1992

I give her the rose with unfurled petals.
She smiles
>   and crosses her legs.
I give her the shell with the swollen lip.
She laughs.   I bite
>   and nuzzle her breasts.

> Suniti Namjoshi, "I Give Her the Rose," in Judith
> Barrington, ed., *An Intimate Wilderness,* 1991

I t's passion, not mere sex, that is the sure foundation of lesbian
identity.

> Gillian Hanscombe, in Judith Barrington, ed., *An
> Intimate Wilderness,* 1991

I am as womanly as I could be. With my lovers, I'm completely a woman. My body is completely a woman's body. When you get to know me, I'm a total woman. I think the male thing is just a way of surviving – outside.

> k.d. lang, in an interview in *The Advocate,* June 16, 1992

Lesbians have arrived at the place where men were in the 70s, before AIDS hit. We're bursting out in our sexual freedom, we're hedonistic, women are rejoicing in the range of their sexuality.

> Katherine Forrest, quoted in *Lambda Book Report,* January/February 1993

There was a refusal to believe a woman could be a sexual object. You kind of hold hands, sing songs. There was supposed to be nothing raw, nothing passionate about what happened between two women. Those of us who wanted to have an erotic life said, "What's wrong with having fantasies and identifying yourself as sexual actors?" It became hotly contested.

> Amber Hollibaugh, on how the definition of lesbian-feminist sexuality began to change in the 1980s, quoted in *New York,* May 10, 1993

FIDELITY

If you remember the power you have over me, you will also remember that I have been in possession of your love for twelve years; I belong to you so utterly, that it will never be possible for you to lose me; and only when I die shall I cease loving you.

> Christina, Queen of Sweden (1626–1689), in a letter to Ebba Sparre, quoted in Margaret Goldsmith, *Christina of Sweden,* 1935

A woman: take her or leave her, but do not take her and leave her.

> Natalie Barney, *Éparpillements,* 1910

It is not sensuality that ensures the fidelity of two women but a kind of blood kinship ... I have written kinship where I should have said identity. Their close resemblance guarantees similarity in volupté. The lover takes courage in her certainty of caressing a body whose secrets she knows, whose preferences her own body has taught her.

> Sidonie Gabrielle Colette, *Ces plaisirs,* 1932

For an instant, in the great blackness which filled the room, a whirling blackness under the wall of water, Margaret thought that they were children again, running ahead of the storm, she with her hand in Susan's. "We'll stick together!" cried Susan, and her voice had the golden curl of a trumpet. "Till we die!" If it was fear that Margaret felt, it had, at the last, the strong sweet taste of great elation.

> Helen R. Hull, "Last September," 1939, *Last September,* 1988

UNION

In their youthful days, they took each other as companions for life, and this union, no less sacred to them than the tie of marriage, has subsisted, in uninterrupted harmony, for 40 years, during which they have shared each others' occupations and pleasures and works of charity while in health, and watched over each other tenderly in sickness ... They slept on the same pillow and had a common purse, and adopted each others' relations...

> William Cullen Bryant, describing a "female friendship" he observed in Vermont, in the *Evening Post,* July 13, 1843. Quoted in Lillian Faderman, *Odd Girls and Twilight Lovers,* 1991

On the whole, it was a necessary and beneficent part. Rosa Bonheur could never have remained the celebrated artist she was without some one beside her, at each instant, to spare her the material cares of the household, the daily worries of existence, and to help her also with moral and physical support, as well as wi.h advice in many things related to her art. Nathalie made herself small, ungrudgingly, so that Rosa might become greater.

> Theodore Stanton, ed., on the roles of Nathalie Micas and Rosa Bonheur, who lived together from 1849 until Micas's death in 1889. *Reminiscences of Rosa Bonheur,* 1910

The two girls were usually known by their sur-names, Banford and March. They had taken the farm together, intending to work it all by themselves: that is, they were going to rear chickens, make a living by poultry, and add to this by keeping a cow, and raising one or two young beast ... March was more robust. She had learned carpentry and joinering at the evening classes in Islington. She would be the man about the place.

> D.H. Lawrence, "The Fox," 1922. This story ends on a disturbing note when Henry destroys the women's union, murdering Banford so he may have March to himself. In *The Fox, The Captain's Doll, The Ladybird,* ed. Dieter Mehl, 1992

They were a recognised couple. Con, who sold gloves in a big West-End establishment, was the wife and homemaker; Norah, the typist, was the husband who planned little pleasure trips and kept the accounts and took Con to the pictures.

> Elsie J. Oxenham, *The Abbey Girls Win Through,* 1930

The geniuses came and talked to Gertrude Stein and the wives sat with me.

> Gertrude Stein, *The Autobiography of Alice B. Toklas,* 1933

I dream of a place between your breasts
to build my house like a haven
where I could plant my crops
in your body
an endless harvest

> Audre Lorde, in *Sinister Wisdom,* Spring 1977

SEPARATION AND PARTING

P rayer to my lady of Paphos

Dapple-throned Aphrodite,
eternal daughter of God,
snare-knitter! Don't, I beg you,

cow my heart with grief! Come

> Sappho (b. 612 B.C.?), in *Sappho: A New Transla-
> tion,* trans. Mary Barnard, 1958

Everything pleasant and delightful
Without you seems like mud underfoot.
I shed tears as I used to smile,
And my heart is never glad.
When I recall the kisses you gave me,
And how with tender words you caressed my little breasts,
I want to die
Because I cannot see you.

> From a love letter from one religious woman to
> another in a twelfth-century manuscript at the mon-
> astery of Tegernsee in Bavaria. Quoted in John
> Boswell, *Christianity, Social Tolerance, and Homo-
> sexuality,* 1980

...Susie, will you indeed come home next Saturday, and be my own again, and kiss me as you used to? Shall I indeed behold you, not "darkly, but face to face" or am I *fancying* so, and dreaming blessed dreams from which the day will wake me? I hope for you so much and feel so eager for you, feel that I *cannot* wait, feel that *now* I must have you – that the expectation once more to see your face again, makes me feel hot and feverish, and my heart beats so fast...

> Emily Dickinson, in a letter to Sue Gilbert, June 27, 1852. In *The Letters of Emily Dickinson,* ed. Thomas Johnson and Theodora Ward, 1958

I cannot grow reconciled to the thought of being away from you. Even a day or two is hard ... Dearest, my dearest, it is hard not to have your good night kiss ... God in His Providence has given me this love when I most need it, when I am about to take up crushing responsibilities...

> Mary Woolley, in a letter to Jeannette Marks written just before Woolley became president of Mount Holyoke College on January 1, 1901. Quoted in Anna Mary Wells, *Miss Marks and Miss Woolley,* 1978

You must know, dear, how I long for you all the time, and especially during the last three weeks. There is reason in the habit of married folks keeping together.

> Jane Addams, in a letter to Mary Smith written in 1902, quoted in Allen F. Davis, *American Heroine,* 1973

Here I am at the desk again, all as natural as can be and writing a first letter to you with so much love, and remembering that this is the first morning in more than seven months that I haven't waked up to hear your dear voice and see your dear face. I do miss it very much, but I look forward to no long separation, which is a comfort.

> Sarah Orne Jewett, in a letter to Annie Fields, in *Letters of Sarah Orne Jewett,* ed. Annie Fields, 1911

For sixteen nights I have listened expectantly for the opening of my door, for the whispered "Lushka!" as you entered my room, and tonight I am alone. How can I sleep? This can't go on. We must once and for all take our courage in both hands and go away together.

> Violet Trefusis, in a letter to Vita Sackville-West, July 22, 1918. Quoted in Nigel Nicolson, *Portrait of a Marriage,* 1973

Painful as her partings had been with women lovers, difficult as some of their arguments and disagreements, she felt they'd pushed her forward, in some way, toward honesty and a better understanding of what she wanted and needed – and never toward self-hatred, the continuing legacy of misogyny.

> Barbara Wilson, "Take Louise Nevelson," *Miss Venezuela,* 1979

Every woman I have ever loved has left her print upon me, where I loved some invaluable piece of myself apart from me – so different that I had to stretch and grow in order to recognize her. And in that growing, we came to separation, that place where work begins.

> Audre Lorde, *Zami,* 1982

We had come together like elements erupting into an electric storm, exchanging energy, sharing charge, brief and drenching. Then we parted, passed, reformed, reshaping ourselves the better for the exchange. I never saw Afrekete again, but her print remains upon my life with the resonance and power of an emotional tattoo.

> Audre Lorde, of herself and Afrekete, "Tar Beach,"
> in Barbara Smith, ed., *Home Girls,* 1983

IN MEMORIAM

...How hard it is to be separated from a friend like my Nathalie, whom I loved more and more as we advanced in life; for she had borne, with me, the mortifications and stupidities inflicted on us ... She alone knew me, and I, her only friend, knew what she was worth.

> Rosa Bonheur, in a letter to Madame Auguste Cain after the death of Nathalie Micas, Bonheur's companion, on June 22, 1889. Quoted in Theodore Stanton, ed., *Reminiscences of Rosa Bonheur,* 1910

I watch the arch of her head,
As she turns away from me...
I would I were with the dead,
Drowned with the dead at sea,
All the waves rocking over me!

> Katherine Bradley (whose pseudonym with Edith Cooper is Michael Field), in memory of Edith Cooper. "Caput Tuum ut Carmelus," *Mystic Trees,* 1913, quoted in Mary Sturgeon, *Michael Field,* 1975

Be to her, Persephone,
All the things I might not be;
Take her head upon your knee.
She that was so proud and wild,
Flippant, arrogant and free,
She that had no need of me

> Edna St. Vincent Millay, in memory of Dorothy Coleman, a Vassar classmate, lover, and friend. "Memorial to D.C.," 1918, in *Collected Lyrics of Edna St. Vincent Millay,* 1939

Nineteen forty-one ... On a quiet evening in October, Georgette's life came to its end. Her tawny eyes opened and looked up at us for the last time. Then she sighed gently, and died. She lay in the room where I am now writing, and I sat beside her in the night and held her hand. As the hours passed I imagined I was hearing Chopin's Twentieth Prelude played as I suddenly knew it should be played.

> Margaret Anderson, on the death of Georgette Le-Blanc in October 1941, *The Strange Necessity,* 1969

God keep you until we meet again ... and believe in my love, which is much, much stronger than mere death.

> Radclyffe Hall, in a letter left to her lover, Lady Una Troubridge, which Lady Una discovered after Hall's death on October 7, 1943. Quoted in Lady Troubridge, *The Life and Death of Radclyffe Hall,* 1961

And if God Choose, I Shall But Love Thee Better After Death. Una.

> Lady Una Troubridge, inscription on a commemorative plaque dedicated to Radclyffe Hall, 1943. Quoted in Richard Ormrod, *Una Troubridge,* 1984

Una Vincenzo Troubridge
the friend of
Radclyffe Hall,
with whom she shared a home for nearly
twenty-nine years.

> Lady Una Troubridge left instructions to have this message engraved on a plaque where she and Radclyffe Hall are buried. Lady Una, who died on September 24, 1963, once remarked: "I feel I must leave an unequivocal record of our life and love, just as The Ladies [of Llangollen] did, to cheer and encourage those who come after us..." Quoted in Richard Ormrod, *Una Troubridge,* 1984

And now she is in the vault at the American Cathedral on the Quai d'Orsay – and I'm here alone. And nothing more – only what was. You will know that nothing is very clear with me – everything is empty and blurred.

> Alice B. Toklas, in a letter written July 31, 1946, to Carl and Fania Van Vechten after the death of Gertrude Stein. In *Staying On Alone,* ed. Edward Burns, 1973

Ah Alice what can I send you now? No words can match such a loss, and what consolation can be found amongst Gertrude's things – without so vivifying a presence? Perhaps her works, which you will continue later on, may bring a feeling of accomplishing those duties which you have always filled to the utmost.

> Natalie Barney, in a letter of condolence to Alice B. Toklas upon the death of Gertrude Stein, 1946. Quoted in George Wickes, *The Amazon of Letters,* 1976

They took the Picasso portrait for the Metropolitan ten days ago. It was another parting and completely undid me. Picasso came over to say good bye to it...

> Alice B. Toklas, in a letter written March 16, 1947, to Henry Rago about Picasso's painting of Gertrude Stein. In *Staying On Alone*, ed. Edward Burns, 1973

And I also remembered how Donne had said that each lover's soul is the body of the other. It was an idea that I'd had no time to tell her, but which would have expressed perfectly our reconciliation, which was of age and time and temperament and heart.

> Elizabeth Mavor, *A Green Equinox*, 1973

ETERNITY

You may forget but

Let me tell you
this: someone in
some future time
will think of us

> Sappho (b. 612 B.C.?), in *Sappho: A New Translation*, trans. Mary Barnard, 1958

Our love is part of infinity,
Absolute as death and beauty...
See, our hearts are joined and our hands are united
Firmly in space and in eternity.

> Renée Vivien, "Union," in *The Muse of the Violets*, trans. Margaret Porter and Catherine Kroger, 1977

We are together in your stillness
you have wished us a bonded life

love of my love, i am your breast
arm of my arm, i am your strength
breath of my breath, i am your foot
thigh of my thigh, back of my back

> Judy Grahn, "A Funeral," quoted in *Another Mother Tongue,* 1984

...But now, like a fresh mountain stream, you have entered the course, and again my life is changed. Stay with me, Lykaina, stay with me always. We will make an eternity of poetry and love, not knowing where one ends and the other begins.

> Ellen Frye, Sappho to Lykaina, *The Other Sappho,* 1989

PART III

ISSUES OF SEXUALITY

BISEXUALITY

Except two breeds – the stupid and the narrowly feline – all women have a touch of the Lesbian: an assertion all good non-analytic creatures refute with horror, but quite true: there is always the poignant intensive personal taste, the *flair* of inner-sex, in the tenderest friendships of women. For myself there is no vice in my Lesbian vain.

> Mary MacLane, *I, Mary MacLane,* 1917

Although my leaning toward the male sex was dominant, I also felt frequently drawn toward my own sex – an inclination which I could not correctly interpret until much later on. As a matter of fact I believe that bisexuality is almost a necessary factor in artistic production; at any rate, the tinge of masculinity within me helped me with my work.

> Käthe Kollwitz, diary entry for 1942, in *Diaries and Letters,* ed. Hans Kollwitz, 1956

A short note about bisexuality. You can't have your cake and eat it too. You can't be tied to male privilege with the right hand while clutching to your sister with the left.

> Rita Mae Brown, in *Sisters,* October 1972

Bisexuality is not so much a copout as a fearful compromise.

> Jill Johnston, *Lesbian Nation,* 1973

If you swing both ways, you really swing. I just figure you double your pleasure.

> Joan Baez, quoted in *Sappho,* May 1973

Bisexuality does not consist in being heterosexual and homo-sexual at the same time, that is, in leading a double life ... rather it consists in being with another, a woman with a man, in a state of dynamic exchange which is so intense, an oscillation of this exchange which is so rapid, in desires which are so strong, that the very process of crossing toward and through the other is made possible...

> Hélène Cixous, in an interview in George Stam-bolian and Elaine Marks, eds., *Homosexualities and French Literature,* 1979

I do believe deeply that all human beings, male and female, are sexual beings, most likely bisexual beings channeled this way and that by cultures terrified of boundary crossings without passports stamped GAY or STRAIGHT.

> Robin Morgan, *The Anatomy of Freedom,* 1982

From a cursory examination of bisexuality in women, we see that female sexual orientation, at least for some, can be fluid and dynamic, and that by implication lesbianism is a multifactored life-style, not merely the expression of a biological imperative or of some intransient orientation fixed early in childhood.

> Margaret Nichols, in David P. McWhirter, Steph-anie A. Sanders, and June Machover Reinisch, eds., *Homosexuality/Heterosexuality,* 1990

Women who call themselves bisexual − not because they are in transition or are afraid of their Lesbianism − but because they choose to relate sexually to both women and men, are the only women who are really heterosexual. They are the only women who choose to relate to men after having known and experienced our non-compulsory alternative.

> Marilyn Murphy, *Are You Girls Traveling Alone?,* 1991

Despite its prevalence, bisexuality traditionally has not been granted independent status as a category of sexuality. Instead, the behavior has been explained away as a phase.

Anastasia Toufexis, in *Time*, August 17, 1992

I have a lot of sexual fantasies about women, and I enjoy being with women, but by and large I'm mostly fulfilled with a man.

Madonna, quoted in *Vanity Fair*, October 1992

I think the way I am is the way everyone is, but will they admit it? Society says it's not the way to be.

Nona Hendryx, on her bisexuality, 1992, quoted in
The Advocate, October 6, 1992

I've had long-term sexual relationships with both men and women. If that classifies me as a bisexual, then I'm bisexual. I'm very committed to people, so when I'm with somebody, I'm *with* them.

Sandra Bernhard, in an interview in *The Advocate*,
December 15, 1992

Bisexual women are and always have been part of the lesbian community.

Rebecca Ripley, in Elizabeth R. Weise, ed., *Closer
to Home*, 1992

Bi-feminists are the women most likely to pioneer a new, inclusive feminist perspective beyond the dualism that lesbian feminism has not yet transcended. After all, we must resolve the duality of gay versus straight within ourselves to come out as bi.

Beth Elliot, in Elizabeth R. Weise, ed., *Closer to
Home*, 1992

Many people deny that bisexuality exists. I happen to feel that women have a natural capacity for bisexuality.

> Camille Paglia, "The M.I.T. Lecture: Crisis in American Universities," *Sex, Art, and American Culture,* 1992

...Obviously the problem for her is that she also now and then dates men. I would like her to be able to say, "Look, *so?* I'm not comfortable with the word 'gay.'" I want her to *say* this. Because I think it's necessary to say. The word *gay* is becoming oppressive. It itself is becoming oppressive. I want her to say this. I want her to say, "I'm not comfortable with that word" – and others like Sandra Bernhard must say it too...

> Camille Paglia, of Jodie Foster, "The M.I.T. Lecture," *Sex, Art, and American Culture,* 1992

HETEROSEXUALITY

Cows do not burn with love for cows, nor mares for mares;
The ram is hot for the ewe, the doe follows the stag.
So also do birds mate, and among all the animals
No female is seized with desire for a female.

> Ovid, lament of a lesbian character in *Metamorphoses,* A.D. 8, quoted in John Boswell, *Christianity, Social Tolerance, and Homosexuality,* 1980

There was a young lady of Trent
To whom a rude postcard was sent.
Its fearful attraction
Caused a major contraction–
The lady, once straight, became bent.

> Limerick #8 in the *Sappho* Limerick Competition, in *Sappho,* March 1974

Gay people have to repress their heterosexuality, though their reasons are very different from the reasons the straight majority repress their homosexual feelings.

> Susan Sontag, in an interview in *Out: The Gay Perspective,* April 1974

An exclusive commitment to one sexual formation, whether homosexual or heterosexual, generally means an exclusive commitment to one role ... An exclusive commitment to one sexual formation generally means that one is, regardless of the uniform one wears, a good soldier of the culture programmed effectively to do its dirty work.

> Andrea Dworkin, *Woman Hating,* 1974

Heterosexuality separates women from each other: it makes women define themselves through men; it forces women to compete against each other for men and the privilege which comes through men and their social standing ... The Lesbian receives none of these heterosexual privileges or compensations ... If she understands her oppression, she has nothing to gain by supporting white rich male America and much to gain from fighting to change it.

> Charlotte Bunch, in Alison M. Jaggar and Paula Rothenberg Struhl, eds., *Feminist Frameworks,* 1978

If you're straight then I'm crooked, but if I'm gay then you're morose.

> Robin Tyler, on her album *Always a Bridesmaid Never a Groom,* 1979

...the existence of lesbianism gives all women the possibility of living heterosexuality with more freedom and less obligations and, ultimately, the possibility of choice.

> "Editorial," in *La Vie en Rose,* June/July/August 1982, quoted in *Lesbian Ethics,* Spring 1986

...I think it's very much harder to be heterosexual, from the inward point of view. It's easier from the social, outer point of view. Of course, I am a lesbian. But if you are a heterosexual woman, you are taking the stranger in; you are taking into you, even physically, somebody very different from you...

> May Sarton, in an interview in Margaret Cruik-shank, ed., *The Lesbian Path*, 1985

There was another kind of lesbian, though, another lesbian history, where the woman did not know, or only knew somewhere in the locked attic of her own elusive mind, for years. This woman lived two lives in her lifetime: first the heterosexual, then the homosexual, the second as if by solemn choice and not by chance or chemistry.

> Sheila Ortiz Taylor, *Spring Forward, Fall Back*, 1985

My lesbianism is not linked to sexual preference ... I do not deny myself heterosexuality or my fascination with a certain kind of male energy.

> Holly Near, *Fire in the Rain*, 1990

Heterosexuality can never fully ignore the close psychical proximity of its terrifying (homo)sexual other, any more than homosexuality can entirely escape the equally insistent social pressures of (hetero)sexual conformity.

> Diana Fuss, in Fuss, ed., *Inside/Out*, 1991

I Can't Even Think Straight

> Message on a shirt spotted in New York City, 1992

I'm straight. But not narrow.

> Message on a pin spotted at the Lambda Rising bookstore in Washington, D.C., 1993

Another Lesbian for Straight Women's Rights
> Message on a pin spotted at Judith's Room book-
> store in New York City, 1993

HOMOSEXUALITY

Homosexual desire is specific; there are homosexual utterances. But homosexuality is nothing; it's only a word. So let's take the word seriously, let's go with it and make it yield all the possibilities it contains.
> Gilles Deleuze, quoted in George Stambolian and
> Elaine Marks, eds., *Homosexualities and French
> Literature,* 1979

The opposition of the sexes must not be a law of Nature; therefore the confrontations and paradigms must be dissolved, both the meanings and the sexes be pluralized ... and sex will be caught in no typology (there will be, for example, only *homosexualities,* whose plural will baffle any constituted, centered discourse, to the point where it seems ... virtually pointless to talk about it).
> Roland Barthes, quoted in George Stambolian and
> Elaine Marks, eds., *Homosexualities and French
> Literature,* 1979

...Sexual orientation is only one aspect of homosexuality, which is really a personality, a sensitivity. A spirit. It cannot be ignored like a pimple or repressed like the urge to eat a chocolate-covered cherry; it cannot be isolated from one's personality.
> Richard Friedel, *The Movie Lover,* 1981

TO BE OR NOT TO BE

After a thorough self-examination, in the light of all I had read and heard about dykes and bull-daggers, I reasoned that I had none of the obvious traits – I didn't wear trousers, or have big shoulders or go in for sports, or walk like a man or even want to touch a woman.

> Maya Angelou, *I Know Why the Caged Bird Sings*, 1969

One may be homosexual for a minute, an hour, a day, or a lifetime.

> George Weinberg, *Society and the Healthy Homosexual*, 1972

Sure, yes, if I only had the time. As it is, I'm working so hard, I barely get in one good fuck a week.

> Shirley MacLaine, on whether she would have an affair with a woman, 1976, quoted in *The Advocate*, October 6, 1992

I'm not a homosexual and I don't smoke pot, so what would I say?

> Lillian Carter, in response to an invitation to appear on *The Phil Donahue Show*, February 24, 1985. Quoted in Leigh W. Rutledge, *The Gay Decades*, 1992

W.H. Auden said he was a poet only when he was writing a poem. We don't yet have the political freedom to be able to be homosexuals only when we are making love with members of our own sex, but it is that freedom I know I'm working for.

> Jane Rule, *A Hot-Eyed Moderate*, 1985

A female lover would have to look exactly like me to really turn me on.

> Roseanne Arnold, 1991, quoted in *The Advocate,* October 6, 1992

It isn't that I hadn't ever considered it. I'd say, "Well, would that be interesting? Would I want to?" And I honestly don't think that the thought ever resolved itself.

> Julie Andrews, on a potential lesbian relationship, quoted in *The Advocate,* October 6, 1992

I don't think she would have called herself a lesbian. But she loved women.

> Maria Riva, of her mother, Marlene Dietrich, quoted in *The Advocate,* March 9, 1993

I hear that Hillary Clinton did have an affair in college with one of us, but don't worry, she didn't inhale.

> Robin Tyler, at the March on Washington for Lesbian, Gay, and Bi Equal Rights, April 25, 1993

PASSING THE LOVE OF MEN

"I assure you, with a love 'passing the Love of Men,' that I am yours..."

> William Hayley, Lucy to Harriot, *The Young Widow,* 1789

 B urnt ... Mr. Montagu's farewell verses that no trace of any man's admiration may remain. It is not meet for me. I love, & only love, the fairer sex & thus beloved by them in turn, my heart revolts from any other love than theirs.

> Anne Lister, diary entry for January 29, 1821, in *I Know My Own Heart*, ed. Helena Whitbread, 1988

... G ladly, gratefully Antoinette welcomed her advent, and the rush of emotion which she had called forth; turned with relief from her fruitless search in the world of masculinity, to give herself up to whole-hearted worship of this proud silent woman...

> A.T. Fitzroy (pseudonym of Rose Laure Allatini), *Despised and Rejected*, 1918. Antoinette falls in love with Hester and sees nothing "unusual about her attitude." Several months after its publication, this book was condemned as morally unhealthy and copies were seized.

 M odern woman is no longer satisfied to be the beloved of a man; she looks for understanding, comradeship; she wants to be treated as a human being and not simply as an object for sexual gratification. And since man in many cases cannot offer her this, she turns to her sisters.

> Emma Goldman, in *Yearbook for Sexual Intermediate Types*, 1923

 W ent out last night with a crowd of my friends,
They must've been women, 'cause I don't like no men...

> Ma Rainey, from the song "Prove It on Me Blues," 1928, reissued on the album *AC-DC Blues: Gay Jazz Reissues*

for she needs no man,
herself
is that dart and pulse of the male,
hands, feet, thighs,
herself perfect.

> Hilda Doolittle, "The Master" (Part V), 1930s?, in
> *H.D.: Collected Poems 1912–1944,* ed. Louis L.
> Martz, 1983

When you see two women walking hand in hand,
Just look 'em over and try to understand:
They'll go to those parties – have the lights down low–
Only those parties where women can go.
You think I'm lying – just ask Jack Ann–
Took many a broad from many a man.

> Bessie Smith, from the song "The Boy in the Boat,"
> 1930

"Otoko, you're all I want. Only you."
    In silence Otoko wiped the cold perspiration from her forehead. "If you go on like that you'll end up unhappy for the rest of your life."
    "I'm not afraid of unhappiness."
    "You're young and pretty, so you can say that."
    "As long as I can be with you I'll be happy."
    "I'm glad – but after all, I'm a woman."
    "I hate men."

> Yasunari Kawabata, *Beauty and Sadness,* 1961

"I don't see what women see in other women," I'd told Doctor Nolan in my interview that noon. "What does a woman see in a woman that she doesn't see in a man?"
    Doctor Nolan paused. Then she said, "Tenderness."

> Sylvia Plath, *The Bell Jar,* 1966

"I hate men," said Priscilla.

"So you've come back to me," said Ada.

"It looks that way," said Priscilla.

In the quiet of the country night they were together again, arms around each other, and they remembered that one, Ada, was to perform the act of kissing.

John O'Hara, *The Ewings,* 1972

"I mean men bore me. If one of them behaves like an adult it's cause for celebration, and even when they do act human, they still aren't as good in bed as women."

Rita Mae Brown, Molly to Polina, *Rubyfruit Jungle,* 1973

Course it ain't quite that simple, so I better explain
Just why you've got to ride on the lesbian train
'Cause if you wait for the man to straighten out your head
You'll all be a-waitin', then you'll all be dead.

Alix Dobkin, from the song "Talking Lesbian," on the album *Lavender Jane Loves Women,* 1975

GIRLS WILL BE BOYS

You frown upon your gentle sex,
And mannish traits assume;
With Nature's perfect harmony
You're sadly out of tune.
Just be content to be yourself
And here, for thought is food,
The greatest gift of God to Man
Is gentle Womanhood.

"The Mannish Maid," on a postcard postmarked 1910, reproduced in Jonathan Katz, *Gay/Lesbian Almanac,* 1983

The sound of trumpets died away and Orlando stood stark naked. No human being since the world began, has ever looked more ravishing. His form combined in one the strength of a man and a woman's grace ... Orlando had become a woman – there is no denying it. But in every other respect, Orlando remained precisely as he had been.

> Virginia Woolf, whose sometimes lover, Vita Sackville-West, was the inspiration for the character Orlando. *Orlando,* 1928

Girls Will
Be Boys.
You Know.

> Message on a postcard from the 1920s, reproduced in Jonathan Katz, *Gay/Lesbian Almanac,* 1983

Colette's understanding of the male sex amounted to an amazing identification with men per se, to which was added her own uterine comprehension of woman, more objective than feminine.

> Janet Flanner, in the Introduction to Sidonie Gabrielle Colette, *Ces plaisirs,* 1932

She saw herself as a queer little girl, aggressive and awkward because of her shyness; a queer little girl who loathed sisters and dolls, preferring the stable-boys as companions, preferring to play with footballs and tops, and occasional catapults. She saw herself climbing the tallest beech trees, arrayed in old breeches illicitly come by. She remembered insisting with tears and some temper that her real name was William and not Wilhelmina.

> Radclyffe Hall, *Miss Ogilvy Finds Herself,* 1934

What is this love we have for the invert, boy or girl? It was they who were spoken of in every romance that we ever read. The girl lost, what is she but the prince found? The prince on the white horse that we have always been seeking. And the pretty lad who is a girl, what but the prince-princess in pointlace – neither one and half the other ... for in the girl it is the prince, and in the boy it is the girl that makes a prince a prince — and not a man.

Djuna Barnes, *Nightwood,* 1936

By the time I was six I was sure that I was born a man.

Carson McCullers, to Louis Untermeyer, 1940, quoted by Virginia Spencer Carr in the Introduction to *Collected Stories of Carson McCullers,* 1987

What irony that many of us choose
To ape that which by nature we despise,
Appear ridiculous to others' eyes
By travelling life's path in borrowed shoes.

How willingly we go with tresses shorn
And beauty masked in graceless, drab attire.
A rose's loveliness is to admire;
Who'd cut the bloom and thus expose the thorn?...

Lisa Ben, "Protest," in *Vice Versa,* January 1948

She thought that homosexual women were great strong creatures in slacks with brush cuts and deep voices; unhappy things, standouts in the crowd. She looked back at herself hugging her bosom as if to comfort herself, and she thought, "I don't want to be a boy. I don't want to be like them. I'm a *girl.* I *am* a girl. That's what I want to be. But if I'm a girl why do I love a girl?

Ann Bannon, describing Laura's dilemma, *Odd Girl Out,* 1957

What if you'd been raised as a boy and learned to be a man, and had to do it all inside a female body? What if you had all your feelings incarcerated under a pair of breasts? What would you do with yourself? How could you live? Who would be your lover?

Ann Bannon, describing Beebo's dilemma, *Beebo Brinker,* 1962

...for status reasons, the male rejects his feminine identification and becomes anxious about the homosexuality it symbolizes; the female, on the other hand, readily accepts her masculine identification, since she aspires to be a man, and, therefore, has little reason to be anxious about the homosexuality that is symbolically associated with it.

> Lionel Ovesey, *Homosexuality and Pseudohomosexuality*, 1969

It's odd being queer.
It's not that you don't want a man,
You just don't want a man in a man.
You want a man in a woman.
The woman-part goes without saying.

> Cherríe Moraga, Marisa to Amalia, *Giving Up the Ghost*, 1986

I discarded a whole book because the leading character wasn't on my wavelength. She was a lesbian with doubts about her masculinity.

> Peter DeVries, quoted in William Cole and Louis Phillips, eds., *Sex: "The Most Fun You Can Have without Laughing" and Other Quotations*, 1990

BUTCH/FEMME RELATIONSHIPS

She is the clinging vine type who is often thought and spoken of by her elders as a little fool without any realization of the warped sexuality which is prompting her actions ... She is more apt to be bisexual and also apt to respond favorably to treatment.

> Frank S. Caprio, of the femme, *Female Homosexuality*, 1954

Someday I expect the "discrete" lesbian will not turn her head on the streets at the sight of the "butch" strolling hand in hand with her friend in their trousers and definitive haircuts. But for the moment it still disturbs.

> Lorraine Hansberry, in *The Ladder,* May 1957, quoted in Marjorie Garber, *Vested Interests,* 1992

The Greatest Pleasure of Them All is a Bath with Butch.

> Advertisement for Butch Bath Oil, a product of the Butch Bath Company, Beverly Hills, in *One: The Homosexual Viewpoint,* March 1963

While she thinks directly and to the point, like a man, she has the endurance and resilience of the female. Her masculinity is often so formidable that it alienates not only the casual male but the very femme she is trying to influence.

> Jess Stearn, of the butch, *The Grapevine,* 1964

Studs as a result of having attained the ultimate in homosexuality (as is perceived by members of this group) are therefore privileged with a higher status within the subculture than that which is accorded the fish, who on the other hand enjoy the situation of marginality.

> Ethel Sawyer, of studs (butches) and fish (femmes), "A Study of a Public Lesbian Community," Washington University, Sociology-Anthropology Essay Series, September 1965

Well, honey, when I went to [Greenwich Village in the early 1960s], there was lesbians in the streets in droves. Women that looked like men, men that looked like women. Women with their hair slicked back, the femmes with the beehives ... I found myself a girlfriend; she was a femme type. And I loved it...

> Red Jordan Arobateau, quoted in Andrea Weiss and Greta Schiller, *Before Stonewall,* 1988

The butch wears fly-front trousers, men's shirts and flat shoes, her clothes conceal her breasts and buttocks, and she may bind her breasts to flatten them. Her hair is cropped short, and she wears cuff links and other male accessories. She always holds the femme's coat, opens doors for her, lights her cigarettes.

Arno Karlen, *Sexuality and Homosexuality,* 1971

My sisters called to me, "Hi, Butch!"
and it hurt
I felt it as a condemnation
and wanted to protest no no
I'm not that masculine woman

Fran Winant, "Dyke Jacket," 1973, in Elly Bulkin and Joan Larkin, eds., *Lesbian Poetry,* 1981

The "butch" may dress and act like a man, but this is simply mimicry in the reverse manner of the effeminate male homosexual. These women proclaim their dislike for maleness, especially penises, and, in the extreme, state that men have value only as repositories of sperm. In sexual relations they take up the masculine role...

Encyclopaedia Britannica, 15th edition, 1974, quoted in *Focus: A Journal of Gay Women,* June 1975

If our double standard proclaimed the sexes to be different but equal, I think that lesbians and male homosexuals who manifested "opposite sex characteristics" would be treated with equal disdain. However, our double standard is that males are superior to females. Therefore, we look with disgust upon the "faggot" who has traded his alleged superior status as a man for the alleged lowly condition of a woman. We can better understand why the "butch" behaves as she does: she is "stepping up."

A.P. MacDonald, Jr., in *Homosexuality Counseling Journal,* October 1974

I call myself a born-again butch. Which means I still have the choreography but I don't do the dance. That's why I wear tuxedo and leather jackets on stage. These women are coming to see me, and through my humour I hope to make it okay to be a butch.

Robin Tyler, quoted in *Sappho* 7(9), 1980

A great deal of public ridicule and embarrassment came down on a butch who "went femme," mainly because of the demeaning social attitudes towards femaleness.

Merrill Mushroom, in *Common Lives, Lesbian Lives,* Autumn 1983

Fems were deeply cherished and yet devalued as well. There were always fem put-down jokes going around the bar, while at the same time tremendous energy and caring was spent courting the fem women...

Joan Nestle, in Carole Vance, ed., *Pleasure and Danger,* 1984

...the butch is, ceremoniously speaking, Puck. Cross-dressing is a magical function, and the butch is the equivalent of the traditional cross-dresser who may also become a magical/shaman of the tribe. She is the one who cross-dresses, becomes a hunter or a sooth-sayer or a prophet or the first woman in a formerly all-male occupation. She keeps the idea of biological destiny untenable.

Judy Grahn, *Another Mother Tongue,* 1984

Because femmes – in varying degrees – fit more closely the male-created ideal of "real woman" we are more privileged than butches, both in the het world and in Lesbian communities. Because butches have rejected feminine conditioning more completely, they are treated as being more Queer, more suspect, more "unnatural."

Linda Strega, in *Lesbian Ethics,* Fall 1985

Dutch

A female homosexual with mannish or aggressive traits.

> The American Heritage Dictionary, 1985. The word femme does not appear.

Butch-femme relationships, as I experienced them, were complex erotic statements, not phony heterosexual replicas. They were filled with a deeply Lesbian language of stance, dress, gesture, loving, courage, and autonomy.

> Joan Nestle, A Restricted Country, 1987

Baby Butch on Board

> Andrea Natalie, message in a cartoon, Stonewall Riots, 1989

The archetypal lesbian couple – the untouchable stone butch and the femme – is a puzzle of the history of women's sexuality in a culture that perceives women as sexually passive. These butches developed an assertive, aggressive sexual stance, uncommon to women of that period.

> Madeline Davis, quoted in JoAnn Loulan with Sherry Thomas, The Lesbian Erotic Dance, 1990

This [ki-ki] is a familiar term that was frequently used sometimes in a perjorative sense in the 1950s. It's still widely used in some sectors of lesbian culture to describe women who move easily from butch to femme and back again.

> JoAnn Loulan with Sherry Thomas, The Lesbian Erotic Dance, 1990

Being Butch is a Bitch

> Message on a shirt spotted in Philadelphia, 1990

There were ... few butches in the '80s who would entertain the notion that they were men trapped in women's bodies, as butches in the 1950s sometimes did. For many of the neo-butches or -femmes the roles actually had little connection with the idealized butch and femme behaviors of their predecessors ... While distinctions in dress in 1980s butch/femme couples were not unusual, it was also common for both women in the couple to dress in a unisex style or to combine styles.

> Lillian Faderman, *Odd Girls and Twilight Lovers,*
> 1991

Butch Fatale

> Slogan on a shirt seen in New York City, 1992

...the femme woman has been the most ambiguous figure in lesbian history; she is often described as the nonlesbian lesbian, the duped wife of the passing woman, the lesbian who marries.

> Joan Nestle, in Nestle, ed., *The Persistent Desire,*
> 1992

S/M

I am convinced that to use violence against another woman, with or without her "consent," is not the way to reach Nirvana.

> Maryel Norris, in Robin R. Linden, Darlene R.
> Pagano, Diana E.H. Russell, and Susan Leigh Star,
> eds., *Against Sadomasochism,* 1982

What I've found quite jolting in several communities is the impulse to silence and ostracize Lesbian batterers while at the same time providing a forum for Lesbian sadists ... Advocating sadomasochism does not help the Lesbian batterer channel her very powerful energy and rage elsewhere. Instead it tells her that hitting another woman may be OK especially if the other "asks for it."

> Sarah Lucia Hoagland, in Robin R. Linden, Darlene R. Pagano, Diana E.H. Russell, and Susan Leigh Star, eds., *Against Sadomasochism,* 1982

The s/m concept of "vanilla" sex is sex devoid of passion. They are saying that there can be no passion without unequal power ... The linkage of passion to dominance/subordination is the proto-type of the heterosexual image of male-female relationships, one which justifies pornography.

> Audre Lorde, in answer to a question posed by Susan Leigh Star about how sadomasochists use the concept of power. In Robin R. Linden, Darlene R. Pagano, Diana E.H. Russell, and Susan Leigh Star, eds., *Against Sadomasochism,* 1982

S/M lesbians have been forced into a struggle to maintain their membership in the movement, and defend themselves against slander. No major spokeswoman for lesbian S/M has argued for any kind of S/M supremacy, or advocated that everyone should be a sadomasochist. In addition to self-defense, S/M lesbians have called for appreciation for erotic diversity and more open discussion of sexuality.

> Gayle Rubin, in Carole S. Vance, ed., *Pleasure and Danger,* 1984

Jane rode around on a Harley-bike.
To strangers she looked just like a bull dyke.
But at home in bed,
To her lover she pled:
"Get the ribbons. You know what I like."

> Karen Winter, "Lesbian Limerick," on S/M bond-age, in *Common Lives, Lesbian Lives,* Summer 1986

Contrary to myth, women who prefer S/M sex often have close and loving relationships. Traditional erotica distorts S/M in much the same way that it distorts lesbianism.

> Pat Califia, *Sapphistry,* 1988

S/M lesbians can feel isolated and oppressed within the lesbian subculture ... Lesbians sometimes patronize gay male leather bars because of this alienation.

> Pat Califia, *Sapphistry,* 1988

Play safe and have fun.

> Cynthia Astuto and Pat Califia, in Pat Califia, ed., *The Lesbian S/M Safety Manual,* 1988

We were camped in [the area for differently abled women] and we were up until 4:00 a.m. trying to find someone to stop the two sadomasochists camped six feet away from us who were whipping each other and using paddles.

> Julia Penelope, on sleepless nights at the Michigan Womyn's Music Festival, quoted in *Outlines,* October 1989

PART IV

KEEPING LESBIANS DOWN

THE CHURCH

God gave them up unto vile affections: for even their women did change the natural use into that which is against nature.

Romans 1:26

He testifies that, God being angry with the human race because of their idolatry, it came about that a woman would desire a woman for the use of foul lust.

St. Ambrose (340?–397), on Romans 1:26, quoted in Louis Crompton, *Journal of Homosexuality,* Fall 1980/Winter 1981

Thus women changed their natural use into that which is against nature, because the women themselves committed shameful deeds with women.

St. Anselm of Canterbury (1033–1109), on Romans 1:26, quoted in Louis Crompton, *Journal of Homosexuality,* Fall 1980/Winter 1981

Clearly [the women] do not mount each other but, rather, offer themselves to the men.

Anastasius, on Romans 1:26, quoted in John Boswell, *Christianity, Social Tolerance, and Homosexuality,* 1980

Against nature, that is, against the order of nature, which created women's genitals for the use of men, and conversely, and not so women could cohabit with women.

Peter Abelard (1079–1142), quoted in Louis Crompton, *Journal of Homosexuality,* Fall 1980/Winter 1981

...the less devout the girl the more likely she is to venture into homosexuality.

> Samuel Kling, *Sexual Behavior and the Law,* 1965

For many reasons – some known, some unknown – men and women have exchanged the truth about God for a lie and have become homosexual. Homosexuality is a choice, a choice to be and do what was not intended.

> Kent Philpott, *The Third Sex? Six Homosexuals Tell Their Stories,* 1975

If homosexuality were the normal way, God would have made Adam and Bruce.

> Anita Bryant, quoted in the *New York Times,* June 5, 1977

We would never advocate a stoning or a burning at the stake, as long as homosexuals keep their sexual preferences to themselves.

> Winnie Mathews, conservative religious delegate at the National Women's Conference in Houston, 1977

I don't hate homosexuals. Yes, the gays have rights – the same rights as any other American who is suffering from a deep personal problem.

> Jerry Falwell, May 3, 1982, quoted in Leigh W. Rutledge, *The Gay Decades,* 1992

We therefore with all reverence and serious intention, in Christ's name, make a public statement: that because these games will bring God's judgement upon us all in this city, we therefore forbid them in the name and authority of Jesus Christ. We believe that they shall not take place. We believe that we live in a democracy and therefore control whatever happens...

> Fundamentalists, from a full-page ad condemning the Gay Games placed in Vancouver dailies, quoted in *Outlines,* January 1990

They want your children.

> Lou Sheldon, in a fundraising letter for his Traditional Values Coalition, 1990, quoted in the *Village Voice,* April 27, 1993

God made no one homosexual ... God makes everyone heterosexual.

> William Consiglio, *Homosexual No More: Practical Strategies for Christians Overcoming Homosexuality,* 1991

Homosexuality makes God vomit.

> Fundamentalist Jay Grimstead, in an interview in *The Advocate,* October 20, 1992

This is a Socialist, antifamily political movement that encourages women to leave their husbands, kill their children, practice witchcraft, destroy capitalism, and become lesbians.

> Pat Robertson, on feminism, in a speech criticizing a proposed Iowa equal-rights amendment, 1992

ON DISCRIMINATION IN THE CHURCH

One should no more deplore "homosexuality" than lefthand-edness ... Surely it is the nature and quality of a relationship that matters: one must not judge it by its outward appearance but by its inward worth. Homosexual affection can be as selfless as heterosexual affection, and, therefore, we cannot see that it is in some way morally worse.

> Alastair Heron, ed., stating the crux of a report by English Quakers who studied homosexuality 1957–1963, *Toward a Quaker View of Sex,* 1963. Quoted in Richard F. Lovelace, *Homosexuality and the Church,* 1978

Self image? What kind of a self image has the church given the Lesbian? Less than human, sinner, celibate, unnatural, perverse, immoral, graceless, shameful, unstable, unworthy, evil-minded, accursed, wicked, impure.

> Del Martin and Phyllis Lyon, *Lesbian/Woman,* 1972

It is only when she can denounce the idiocy of religious scrip-tures and legal strictures that bind her and can affirm her lesbian nature as but a single facet of her whole personality that she can become fully human.

> Del Martin and Phyllis Lyon, *Lesbian/Woman,* 1972

Today Americans are in a state of terminal hysteria on the subject of sex in general and homosexuality in particular because the owners of the country (buttressed by a religion that they have shrewdly adapted to their own ends) regard the family as their last means of control over those who work and consume. For two millennia, women have been treated as chattel, while homosexuality has been made to seem a crime, a vice, an illness.

> Gore Vidal, "Sex Is Politics," *Pink Triangle and Yellow Star and Other Essays 1976–1982,* 1982

I've learned that God doesn't punish people. I've learned that God doesn't dislike homosexuals, like a lot of Christians think. AIDS isn't their fault, just like it isn't my fault. God loves homosexuals as much as He loves everybody else.

> Ryan White, at age 16, at a public forum May 30, 1988, in answer to the question "How does your Christian faith help you with your disease?" Quoted in Leigh W. Rutledge, *The Gay Decades,* 1992

I find it difficult to believe that a church that blesses dogs in a Virginia fox hunt can't find a way to bless life-giving, lasting relationships between human beings.

> John Spong, Episcopal bishop of Newark, New Jersey, 1988

To those of you in the Church who lock your doors to us, telling us we are unworthy sinners I shout: LET MY PEOPLE IN!

> Rose Mary Denman, *Let My People In,* 1990

Shows on lesbians generate, for some reason, a more ferocious reaction from the Bible Belt than any other kind of show. You can do a show about sex on trapezes, and it will generate less of a backlash than a show on lesbians.

> Geraldo Rivera, quoted in *The Advocate,* February 25, 1992

Christ walks with the rejected not rejectors.

> Message on a sign held by a lesbian protester during the 1993 Saint Patrick's Day Parade in New York City, in which lesbians and gay men were forbidden to march under their own banner. Ironically, this same year lesbians and gay men in Dublin were allowed to march for the first time in that city's Saint Patrick's Day Parade.

The Pope runs all over the world condemning homosexuality dressed in high drag. Now I ask you!

> Robin Tyler, at the March on Washington for Lesbian, Gay, and Bi Equal Rights, April 25, 1993

The reason that the Catholic hierarchy focuses on condemning homosexuality is to cover up the disproportionate amount of pedophilia within the Catholic priesthood.

> Robin Tyler, at the March on Washington for Lesbian, Gay, and Bi Equal Rights, April 25, 1993

...to call our opponents the Right states a profound untruth. They are wrong. They are wrong! They are wrong morally. They are wrong spiritually. And they are wrong politically. The Christian supremacists are wrong spiritually when they demonize us. They are wrong when they reduce the complexity and beauty of our spirit to a freak show. They are wrong spiritually because if we are the untouchables of America, if we are the untouchables, then we are as Mahatma Gandhi said, children of God.

> Urvashi Vaid, in a speech at the March on Washington for Lesbian, Gay, and Bi Equal Rights, April 25, 1993

PSYCHIATRISTS AND PSYCHOLOGISTS

It merely requires that the right instruction, the right environment, the right opportunities be afforded, and thousands of
women and girls, who now follow lesbian practices might once
more become normal individuals. They might even become
happy wives and mothers, if only their mental condition could be
corrected by therapeutic or normal suggestion, and their endo-
crine system toned up by administration of such extracts as would
enhance their feminine characteristics and reactions ... Some we
would probably kill. Others we would cure.

> La Forest Potter, *Strange Loves: A Study in Sexual
> Abnormalities,* 1933

Psychoanalytical experience teaches us that the unconscious
reason for female homosexuality is to be found in an unsolved
oral-masochistic conflict of the pre-Oedipal child with the mother.

> Edmund Bergler, *Neurotic, Counterfeit-Sex: Impo-
> tence, Frigidity, Mechanical and Pseudosexuality,
> Homosexuality,* 1951

...lesbians who seek psychiatric treatment are, for the most part,
conscientious in wanting to control their compulsive needs for
homosexual gratifications. While every psychoanalyst has in-
stances where lesbians continue to engage in homosexual practices
during and after treatment, the majority of them report with pride
that psychoanalysis has enabled them to make an adequate
heterosexual adjustment.

> Frank S. Caprio, *Female Homosexuality,* 1954

Crime is intimately associated with female sexual inversion.
Many crimes committed by women, upon investigation, reveal
that the women were either confirmed lesbians who killed be-

cause of jealousy or were latent homosexuals with a strong aggressive masculine drive.

> Frank S. Caprio, *Female Homosexuality,* 1954

Women with unrecognized homosexual tendencies may produce profound effects on their husbands' creative, productive, and functional abilities – economically, socially and sexually. Consumed by love for their homosexual partners, they shunt aside all other considerations.

> Charles W. Socarides, in Ralph Slovenko, ed., *Sexual Behavior and the Law,* 1965

Homosexuality is a disturbing word. No one, not even the affected individual, really relishes what it describes.

> John R. Cavanaugh, *Counseling the Invert,* 1966

...despite propaganda to the contrary, there is no such thing as a well-adjusted, happy homosexual.

> George Kriegman, in the *Journal of School Health,* May 1969

...It appears probable that homosexuals are disproportionately involved in both suicide and homicide. The narcissistic homosexual is apparently better suited to take human life – whether his own or another's.

> Paul Cameron, in the *Human Life Review,* Summer 1978

Buried under the "gay" exterior of the homosexual is the hurt and rage that crippled his or her capacity for true maturation, for healthy growth and love.

> Robert Kronemeyer, *Overcoming Homosexuality,* 1980

ANOTHER VIEW FROM
PSYCHIATRISTS AND PSYCHOLOGISTS

The Gay Liberation movement is the best therapy the homosexual has had in years.

> Lawrence Leshan, February 28, 1971, quoted in Barbara Bennett and Linda Amster, eds., *Who Said What (and When and Where and How) in 1971,* 1972

In reviewing my experiences with lesbian clients, I see them struggling with the same issues as other people: that is, how to live self-actualizing lives through gaining a strong sense of self-esteem, establishing and maintaining meaningful relationships, and pursuing satisfying work. There is no particular psychotherapy for lesbians, but, rather, psychotherapy with women who happen to be lesbian.

> Bronwyn D. Anthony, in the *Journal of Homosexuality,* Winter 1981/Spring 1982

...Women who have, at some time in their lives, participated in a sexual experience with another woman ... [are] more satisfied with their bodies and body functions, more satisfied with both their sexual activities and their biological sex, and more satisfied with themselves and their abilities.

> Ronald A. LaTorre and Kristina Wendenburg, in Michael W. Ross, ed., *Homosexuality and Social Sex Roles,* 1983

Clearly, much counseling of lesbians and gay men would not be necessary if broader societal views of homosexual orientation were more positive.

> Stephen F. Morin, in the *Counseling Psychologist,* April 1991

For lesbians of all colors, as well as for all men and women of color, the development of identity is quite complex ... This developmental process will most likely mandate periods of conflict and separation as those who are "different" struggle to incorporate their experience of subordination to and rejection by the standards of society.

Oliva M. Espin and Mary Ann Gawelek, in Laura S. Brown and Mary Ballou, eds., *Personality and Psychopathology*, 1992

THE MILTARY

JOHNNIE PHELPS: Yessir. If the General pleases I will be happy to do this investigation ... But, sir, it would be unfair of me not to tell you, my name is going to head the list ... You should also be aware that you're going to have to replace all the file clerks, the section heads, most of the commanders, and the motor pool ... I think you should also take into consideration that there have been no illegal pregnancies, no cases of venereal disease, and the General himself has been the one to award good conduct commendations and service commendations to these members of the WAC detachment.

GENERAL EISENHOWER: Forget the order.

Johnnie Phelps, World War II WAC sergeant, in response to a request from General Eisenhower that she ferret out the lesbians in her battalion. Related in an interview with Bunny MacCulloch, 1982, quoted in Lillian Faderman, *Odd Girls and Twilight Lovers*, 1991

The Creator has endowed the bodies of women with the noble mission of motherhood and the bringing of human life into the world. Any woman who violates this great trust by participating in homosexuality not only degrades herself socially but also destroys the purpose for which God created her.

> From the Indoctrination Lectures on Homosexuality presented to WAVE (Navy) recruits in 1952. Quoted in Allan Bérubé and John D'Emilio, "The Military and Lesbians during the McCarthy Years," in E. Freedman, B. Gelpi, S. Johnson, and K. Weston, eds., *The Lesbian Issue: Essays from Signs,* 1985

If a woman Marine is a little too friendly, she's a slut. If she doesn't smile at all, she's a dyke. I personally believe that a woman Marine in the normal course of a day confronts more stress and more bullshit than a male Marine would in twenty years.

> Captain Guy Richardson, in *The Progressive,* March 1989

I understand that homosexuality is incompatible with military service and that I may be disenrolled from my program for this reason. A homosexual is defined as a person, regardless of sex, who engages in, desires to engage in, or intends to engage in homosexual acts. A homosexual act means bodily contact, actively undertaken or passively permitted between members of the same sex for the purpose of satisfying sexual desires.

> Excerpt from an affidavit of the Navy's Reserve Officers' Training Corps banning homosexuality that all midshipmen are required to sign, 1992

We've got to consider ... the rights of those who are not homosexual and who give up a great deal of their privacy when they go into the military...

> U.S. senator Sam Nunn, 1992, quoted in *Amethyst* (Binghamton), December 1992/January 1993

The Navy has policies against people who are obese, so why shouldn't they be able to get rid of homosexuals?

> A Navy ship repair inspector, quoted in the *New York Times,* January 31, 1993

We must recognize that women who are targets for female homosexuals experience a unique form of sexual harassment which can be even more devastating ... than the more traditional harassment from men.

> Vice Admiral of the Navy, quoted in the *Village Voice,* April 27, 1993

ON DISCRIMINATION IN THE MILITARY

Military men, from the bottom ranks to the top, don't want women in their midst and the most expedient way to get rid of women — whether they can be gay women or married heterosexuals with children — is to pin them with the label "lesbian."

> Lisa M. Keen, in the *Washington Blade,* March 10, 1989

I was more comfortable with lesbians. Lesbians tend to be rougher, tougher, tomboyish types. I came across good heterosexual marines, but the majority were a bunch of little makeup-wearing prissies. With lesbians, I could swear up a storm, drink beer, burp.

> Barbara Baum, a former marine who was court-martialed for having lesbian sex and served six months in prison. Baum has said she is not a lesbian. Quoted in *The Advocate,* April 25, 1989

...lesbians are especially hard hit by the military policy. Of all the discharges from the Marine Corps, for example, a woman is seven times more likely than a man to have been removed for homosexuality.

New York Times, November 15, 1992

To be granted that right [to serve in the military] does not mean an end to the subjugation of homosexuals, but it is the beginning of civil dignity and equal responsibility.

The Editors, "Ending the Ban," in the *New Republic,* December 7, 1992

Apple pie, motherhood, and the American flag will not fall. We're already in the military.

Miriam Ben-Shalom, quoted in *The Advocate,* December 29, 1992

First I ask myself: Do I trust the safety of my country to women? Well, yes. I know that they're quite capable, quite mean, quite everything. And I feel the same way again about gay men or gay women – the meanest fuckers in the world. I feel wholly secure with them guarding the country. Seriously. They've had the best parades.

Tom Arnold, in an interview with Tom and Roseanne Arnold in *The Advocate,* March 9, 1993

Heroism, I believe, is a trait that does not know race, color, creed, sex, or sexual orientation.

Dianne Feinstein, on why the ban on lesbians and gay men in the military should be lifted, in *The Advocate,* April 6, 1993

We march because women are discharged from the military three times more than men for allegedly violating this ban, and yet women have been missing in action in Congress. When the Senate Armed Services Committee held their hearings, you could have played a game of what's wrong with this picture.

> Patricia Ireland, on the absence of lesbians in Senate hearings debating the ban on lesbians and gay men in the military. In a speech at the March on Washington for Lesbian, Gay, and Bi Equal Rights, April 25, 1993

I fear for every homosexual right now who's in the military. I fear that they may become another Allen Schindler. And the reason I'm speaking out is because I don't want any more Allen Schindlers. I don't want any mother to ever have to go through what I'm going through.

> Dorothy Hajdys, the mother of Allen R. Schindler, the 22-year-old Navy radioman who was brutally murdered by fellow sailors because he was gay. In a speech at the March on Washington for Lesbian, Gay, and Bi Equal Rights, April 25, 1993

Be all that you can be, queers can do it in the Army

> Romanovsky and Phillips, sung at the March on Washington for Lesbian, Gay, and Bi Equal Rights, April 25, 1993

It is time to shift the focus from status to misconduct. There are thousands of cases of sexual misconduct that have gone unresolved, while our military has spent nearly half a billion dollars separating 16,000 lesbians and gays.

> Edward Kennedy, in an opening statement at the Senate Armed Services Committee hearings debating the ban on lesbians and gay men in the military, March 1993. Quoted in the *Village Voice*, April 27, 1993

In support of our nation, everyone should have the right to bear arms — but not bare feet.

> Kenneth Cole, in an advertisement for his shoes that depicted a gay rights demonstration outside a U.S. Armed Forces recruiting center, 1993

HETEROSEXUAL WOMEN'S FEAR AND INTOLERANCE

Equal political rights; identical professional careers; the man's virile force tamed down to harmony with the woman's feminine weakness; the abolition of all moral and social distinctions between the sexes; — these are the confessed objects of the movement whereby men are to be made lady-like and women masculine, till the two melt into one, and you scarcely know which is which.

> Elizabeth Lynn Linton, *The Autobiography of Christopher Kirkland,* 1885

A form of perversion that is well known among workers in reform schools and institutions for delinquent girls, is that of love-making between the white and colored girls. This particular form of the homosexual relation has perhaps not been brought to the attention of scientists.

> Margaret Otis, in a report in the *Journal of Abnormal Psychology,* 1913

...Crooked, twisted freaks of nature who stagnate in dark and muddy waters, and are so cloaked with the weeds of viciousness and selfish lust that, drained of all pity, they [lesbians] regard their victims as mere stepping stones to their further pleasures. With flower-sweet fingertips they crush the grape of evil till it is exquisite, smooth and luscious to the taste, stirring up subconscious responsiveness, intensifying all that has been, all that follows, leaving their prey gibbering, writhing, sex sodden shadows of their former selves, conscious of only one desire in mind and body, which, ever festering, ever destroying, slowly saps their health and sanity.

Sheila Donisthorpe, *Loveliest of Friends*, 1931

The need for affection may be directed toward the same sex if the way to the other sex is barred by too much anxiety. Needless to say, this anxiety need not be manifest, but may be concealed by a feeling of disgust or disinterest concerning the opposite sex.

Karen Horney, *The Neurotic Personality of Our Time*, 1937

The instability of lesbian life – the jumping from partner to partner – makes adjustment to homosexual life very fragile indeed; so that even when the homosexual does seek treatment, can afford it, is able to find it available in her area, and is persistent enough to benefit from it, there is still tremendous insecurity in her life pattern; there is still anxiety and cynicism in her thinking.

Ann Aldrich, *Carol in a Thousand Cities*, 1960

The label "gay" behind which they hide is a defense mechanism against the emptiness, the coldness, and the futility of their lives.

May E. Romm, in Judd Marmor, ed., *Sexual Inversion*, 1965

There are two very different types of women lobbying for the Equal Rights Amendment. One group is the women's liberationists. Their motive is totally radical. They hate men, marriage, and children. They are out to destroy morality and the family.

Phyllis Schlafly, in the *Phyllis Schlafly Report*, November 1972

However happy physical relations between homosexual women may be, they are deprived of the last stop, and have to come to terms with the void.

> Charlotte Wolff, *Love between Women,* 1972

I won't play lesbians, honey. Not this kid.

> Jane Wyman, 1976, quoted in Amy Appleby, ed., *Quentin Crisp's Book of Quotations,* 1989

Who says homosexuals and Lesbians, flaunting their perverted sexuality, aren't a potential danger to our children? ... Some homosexuals are known to go into jealous rages. The potential danger to our children exists.

> Anita Bryant, in Anita Bryant and Bob Green, *At Any Cost,* 1978

I was actually concerned that I *would* be smooching with Demi Moore. I have just managed to live down the lesbianism of *The Color Purple.*

> Whoopi Goldberg, quoted in *OutWeek,* June 27, 1990

During the last fifteen years I have conducted the analysis of twelve women who were obligatory homosexuals ... In my opinion, the most important clinical finding consisted of the fact that these women suffered a very specific type of developmental arrest. When schematization of the body and its inner representation was being laid down, the vagina and inner space per se were not included. This unhappy turn of events was traceable to chronically disturbed relationships with both parents.

> Elaine V. Siegel, "The Search for the Vagina in Homosexual Women," in Charles W. Socarides and Vamik D. Volkan, eds., *The Homosexualities and the Therapeutic Process,* 1991

ON HETEROSEXUAL WOMEN'S
FEAR AND INTOLERANCE

Straight women fear Lesbians because of the Lesbian inside them, because we represent an alternative.

> Martha Shelly, 1969, in Robin Morgan, ed., *Sisterhood Is Powerful,* 1970

In 1968 we had the demonstration against the Miss America Pageant and one of the vehement cries was "You're all a bunch of dykes!" Of course, the women cried and recoiled and ran home ... during this time there were a lot of purges and backstabbing by so-called straight women who didn't understand who in the hell hurt the lesbian sister sitting next to her.

> Gloria Steinem, in an interview in the *Lesbian Tide,* November 1972

...heterosexual women are really on an ego trip. If they hear a woman's a lesbian, they think – she wants my body! This idea is based on fear and ignorance, just like the idea that male homosexuals are child-molesters.

> Ruth Simpson, in an interview in Kay Tobin and Randy Wicker, *The Gay Crusaders,* 1972

The irrational fear of Lesbianism is used not only to divide us from other women but also to keep all women isolated from each other...

> The Boston Women's Health Book Collective, *Our Bodies, Ourselves,* 1973

Any woman who feels actual horror or revulsion at the thought of kissing or embracing or having physical relations with another woman should reexamine her feelings and attitudes not only about other women, but also about *herself.*

> Shere Hite, *The Hite Report: A Nationwide Study on Female Sexuality,* 1976

We must understand that what we are attempting is a revolution, not a public relations movement. As long as we fear the word "lesbian" we are curtailing our own strength and abandoning our sisters.

> Gloria Steinem, in Ginny Vida, ed., *Our Right to Love,* 1978

To some women "dyke" will always be a four-letter word.

> Rhonda Dicksion, Survival Tip #79, *The Lesbian Survival Manual,* 1990

MORE PATRIARCHAL STICKS AND STONES

If, however, a woman commits this vice or sin against nature, she shall [also] be fastened naked to a stake in the Street of the Locusts and shall remain there all day and night under a reliable guard, and the following day shall be burned outside the city.

> Provision in the statutes of Treviso, Italy, 1574, quoted in Louis Crompton, *Journal of Homosexuality,* Fall 1980/Winter 1981

Unnatural filthiness, to be punished with death, whether sodomy, which is carnal fellowship of man with man, or woman with woman, or buggery...

> Reverend John Cotton, in proposed legislation for the Colony of Massachusetts, 1636, quoted in Jonathan Katz, *Gay/Lesbian Almanac,* 1983

If any man lyeth with mankinde, as a man lyeth with a woman, both of them have committed abomination, they both shall surely be put to death. Levit. 20.13. And if any woman change the naturall use into that which is against nature, as Rom. I, 26, she shall be liable to the same sentence, and punishment.

> New Haven sodomy statute, passed in 1655, quoted in Louis Crompton, *Journal of Homosexuality,* Fall 1980/Winter 1981

The crime of women who corrupt one another is regarded as a kind of sodomy, if they practice venereal acts after the fashion of a man and a woman, and is worthy of capital punishment.

> Daniel Jousse, 1771, quoted in Louis Crompton, *Journal of Homosexuality,* Fall 1980/Winter 1981

...the lesbian is and can only be a sexless being.

> Julien Chevalier, *Inversion sexuelle,* 1893

The female possessed of masculine ideas of independence, the viragint who would sit in the public highways and lift up her pseudo-virile voice, proclaiming her sole right to decide questions of war or religion, or the value of celibacy and the curse of woman's impurity, and that disgusting anti-social being, the female sexual pervert, are simply different degrees of the same class − degenerates.

> William Lee Howard, *The Perverts,* 1901

The two men living together and the two women who are perfectly satisfied with their mutual eroticism will never marry and their lives are of single sexuality. They harm the social order, because their lives are selfish and unproductive. When they die they leave nothing behind but sordid memories.

> David H. Keller, in the pamphlet "Sex and Society," 1928, quoted in the newsletter of the San Francisco Bay Area Gay and Lesbian Historical Society, March 1987

Here is a much-needed book which examines straight-forwardly the dramatic problem of women involved too intimately in one another's lives – a powerful novel of a little known social menace. Read this book, and gain an enlightened understanding of the lost women whose strange urges produce one of the great problems of modern society.

Message on the back cover of *Queer Patterns* by Lilyan Brock, 1935

Lesbian
1. Of or pertaining to the island of Lesbos, in the Grecian archipelago. 2. Lesbian vice, sapphism.

Sapphism
Unnatural sexual relations between women.

The Oxford Universal Dictionary, 1955

There is no more glamor in homosexuality than there is in, let's say, a case of typhoid fever.

Edmund Bergler, *One Thousand Homosexuals: Conspiracy of Silence, or Curing and Deglamorizing Homosexuals?,* 1959

There is little doubt that there is considerable homosexuality among lonesome girls rooming together in a large city, especially if they are of small-town extraction, and unable to adjust to the more complex social life of the metropolis.

Matt Bradley, *Faggots to Burn!,* 1962

...homosexual life is a life of contradictions, a sort of nebulous never-never land where what was true this morning isn't necessarily true this afternoon.

Matt Bradley, *Faggots to Burn!,* 1962

The mothers of homosexuals, once they have been confronted with their sons' or daughters' tragic situation, present a problem of their own, especially for the poor husband. The depressed man immediately finds himself with two patients on his hands, not to mention his own unhappiness.

> Edmund Bergler, *Homosexuality: Disease or Way of Life?*, 1962

Growth of Overt Homosexuality Provokes Wide Concern Condition Can Be Prevented or Cured, Many Experts Say

> Title of an article in the *New York Times*, December 27, 1963

The love that dare not speak its name has become the neurosis that doesn't know when to shut up.

> *Time*, April 3, 1964

Homosexuality, once considered the exclusive province of big cities, has spread its tentacles like an octopus into smaller communities. In these, it is even a more serious problem than in the metropolitan areas because authorities have little experience in coping with it. Many officials in these medium-sized towns choose to ignore it. Others incubate scandals that mushroom to such proportions that the very lives of their communities are endangered.

> Antony James, *America's Homosexual Underground*, 1965

Homosexuality is a sickness, just as are baby-rape or wanting to become head of General Motors.

> Eldridge Cleaver, *Soul on Ice*, 1967

Homosexuality is not admirable. The fact that a substantial minority of the population is, by choice or conditioning, homosexual is an eloquent witness to the tragic disorder of our society. The remedy is not in the threat of punishment; rather it is in the example of a more excellent way.

> Stuart Babbage, in *Sexual Latitude,* 1971

Homosexual practices are believed to occur much less widely among women than among men and seem never to have been thought to constitute so grave a danger to society. There have in fact been only very few cases of violation or seduction of children by women and it is most unusual for homosexual practices between consenting adult women to occur in public places.

> "Lesbianism," *Encyclopedia Britannica,* 1973

Lesbianism has been occasionally practised by small groups of women as a "cult."

> "Lesbianism," *Encyclopedia Britannica,* 1973

...Some professions shouldn't be open to women because they can't handle certain jobs, like construction work. Lesbians, maybe, but not women.

> Muhammad Ali, quoted in *New York Amsterdam News,* January 14, 1978

I don't think homosexuality is normal behavior and I oppose the codification of gay rights. But I wouldn't harrass them and I wish they could know that. Actually I wish the whole issue could be toned down. I wish it could go away...

> George Bush, during his campaign for the Republican presidential nomination, 1980. Quoted in Leigh W. Rutledge, *The Gay Decades,* 1992

We must either defeat militant homosexuality or it will defeat us. They have made it clear: We have no other choice.

> William Dannemeyer (R-CA), in the *Congressional Record,* quoted in *Outlines,* October 1989

I feel the same way about homosexuals as I do about cigarette smokers. I wouldn't want to spend much time in a small room with one but they don't bother me otherwise.

> Syndicated columnist Andy Rooney, quoted in *Outlines,* December 1989

I think it's sick. Hide 'em away. Take 'em to the desert or something, I don't know. I think it's sick. It's sick. I don't know, just get 'em out of here.

> Audience member on *The Donahue Show,* about the gay soap opera *Secret Passions,* March 2, 1990, quoted in *Outlines,* April 1990

Children can be told that gay and lesbian relationships are wrong, but they don't have to hate gays and lesbians.

> A heterosexual male doctor, in a discussion of *Daddy's Roommate* and other gay and lesbian children's books, on the TV show *Larry King Live,* September 11, 1992

Homosexual rights, that's not the kind of change America needs.

> Pat Buchanan, in a speech at the Republican National Convention, 1992

Family Values Forever, "Gay" Rights Never

> Message on signs held by the Republican Youth Program contingent at the Republican National Convention, 1992

ON FORMS OF HOMOPHOBIA

The only unsatisfactory thing about Tommy's return was that she brought with her a girl she had grown fond of at school, a dainty, white, languid bit of a thing, who used violet perfumes and carried a sunshade. The Old Boys said it was a bad sign when a rebellious girl like Tommy took to being sweet and gentle to one of her own sex, the worst sign in the world.

> Willa Cather, "Tommy, the Unsentimental," 1896, in Joan Nestle and Naomi Holoch, eds., *Women on Women,* 1990

I am sure that the impulse of desire towards someone of the same sex is not in itself wrong: it is not an offence in any degree – neither against God nor Man. And although for a short time I took pleasure in thinking I was flouting Society, it was exactly the same degree of pleasure that I felt when I wore a daringly low-cut dress, or first wore trousers and walked in Mecklenburgh Square (in 1926 this was a startling thing to do)...

> Valentine Ackland, *For Sylvia: An Honest Account,* 1985. Ackland had her first lesbian affair in 1922, at age 16.

They would ask if I was a man or a woman. They could arrest a woman for impersonating a man, so you had to be sure you were wearing three pieces of women's clothes. You learned to avoid the police ... It was always in the backs of our minds that we could be arrested. Any woman wearing pants was suspect.

> Jackie, on lesbian life in New Orleans in the 1950s, in a 1987 interview with Lillian Faderman, *Odd Girls and Twilight Lovers,* 1991

...**e**very homosexual and lesbian in this country survives solely by sufferance, not by law or even that cold state of grace known as tolerance.

> Editorial, September 1969, in *Come Out! Selections from the Radical Gay Liberation Newspaper*, 1970

Lesbian is a label invented by the Man to throw at any woman who dares to be his equal, who dares to challenge his prerogatives ... who dares to assert the primacy of her own needs.

> Radicalesbians, "The Woman-Identified Woman," May 1970, in *Come Out! Selections from the Radical Gay Liberation Newspaper*, 1970

One distressing thing is the way men react to women who assert their equality: their ultimate weapon is to call them unfeminine. They think she is anti-male; they even whisper that she is probably a lesbian.

> Shirley Chisholm, *Unbought and Unbossed*, 1970

Lesbian-baiting is, of course, a favorite masculine ploy in putting down feminists.

> Del Martin and Phyllis Lyon, *Lesbian/Woman*, 1972

...**t**he machinery of discrimination against lesbians has been able to grind quietly. By granting numerous social privileges and responsibilities to women only if they married, societies have uniformly punished lesbians without even having to acknowledge that they existed.

> George Weinberg, *Society and the Healthy Homosexual*, 1972

Time stops: the felt pen recording, the magazine, the tape recorders, my terrified mind stops remembering it, while Teresa Juarez's voice loud butches me from a floor mike center of the room, a bully for all the correct political reasons. Five hundred people looking at me. Are you a Lesbian? Everything pauses, faces look up in terrible silence. I hear them not breathe. That word in public, the word I waited half a lifetime to hear. Finally I am accused.

Kate Millett, *Flying*, 1974

...through centuries of suckling men emotionally at our breasts we have also been told that we were polluted, devouring, domineering, masochistic, harpies, butches, dykes, and whores.

Adrienne Rich, *Of Woman Born*, 1976

Lesbians, suffering from the dual disqualification of being gay and female, have been repeatedly dispossessed of their history.

Renée Vivien, *A Woman Appeared to Me*, 1976

"Women are afraid to admit they love each other."
"With good reason. Women can be read out of society very easily."

Sarah Aldridge, 'Bel and Andrea, *All True Lovers*, 1978

Heterosexuality has been both forcibly and subliminally imposed on women. Yet everywhere women have resisted it, often at the cost of physical torture, imprisonment, psychosurgery, social ostracism, and extreme poverty. "Compulsory heterosexuality" was named as one of the "crimes against women" by the Brussels International Tribunal on Crimes against Women in 1976.

Adrienne Rich, "Compulsory Heterosexuality and Lesbian Existence," 1980, *Blood, Bread, and Poetry*, 1986

The lie of compulsory female heterosexuality today afflicts not just feminist scholarship, but every profession, every reference work, every curriculum, every organizing attempt, every relationship or conversation over which it hovers. It creates, specifically, a profound falseness, hypocrisy, and hysteria in the heterosexual dialogue, for every heterosexual relationship is lived in the queasy strobe light of that lie.

> Adrienne Rich, "Compulsory Heterosexuality and Lesbian Existence," 1980, *Blood, Bread, and Poetry,* 1986

The denial of reality and visibility to women's passion for women, women's choice of women as allies, life companions and community; the forcing of such relationships into dissimulation and their disintegration under intense pressure, have meant an incalculable loss to the power of all women ... *to liberate ourselves and each other.*

> Adrienne Rich, "Compulsory Heterosexuality and Lesbian Existence," 1980, *Blood, Bread, and Poetry,* 1986

...One feature of lesbian oppression consists precisely of making women out of reach for us, since women belong to men. Thus a lesbian *has* to be something else, a not-woman, a not-man, a product of society, not a product of nature, for there is no nature in society.

> Monique Wittig, "One Is Not Born a Woman," 1981, *The Straight Mind and Other Essays,* 1992

It's hard for young people today (1982) to imagine that as little as 20 years ago a hundred gay people were sitting around arguing over whether or not they should say that they weren't mentally ill.

> Craig Rodwell, quoted in Andrea Weiss and Greta Schiller, *Before Stonewall,* 1988

It had first spread through the block like a sour odor that's only faintly perceptible and easily ignored until it starts growing in strength from the dozen mouths it had been lying in ... And then it was everywhere — lining the mouths and whitening the lips of everyone as they wrinkled up their noses at its pervading smell, unable to pinpoint the source...

> Gloria Naylor, on the spread of homophobia, *The Women of Brewster Place,* 1983

I pounded on my car and screamed, "They misspelled it! They misspelled it!" For some reason, that offended me more than anything else.

> Elaine Noble, after finding "LESBEAN" scrawled on her vehicle, 1984, quoted in *The Advocate,* October 6, 1992

It is Taboo for women Intimately/Ultimately to Touch each other.

> Mary Daly, *Pure Lust,* 1984

When homophobia wins, all women lose.

> Suzanne Pharr, *Homophobia: A Weapon of Sexism,* 1988

Oddly, the homosexual is a far more threatening figure than the androgyne. Society after society has passed laws against homosexuals, but not against androgynes. Homosexuals are more menacing, in part simply because they exist.

> Catharine R. Stimpson, *Where the Meanings Are,* 1988

Where sexism and homophobia meet, you get a viciousness the likes of which you have never seen.

> Sandra Lowe, at Yale University, October 28, 1989

Historically, societies that have condemned the woman who is lesbian have dealt with her in several ways. At times they have tried to destroy her: by burning her at the stake, by hanging her, by guillotining her. At times they have tried to "cure" her: by asking her to remove from her life any type of eroticism, or by asking her to change her erotic orientation.

Dolores Klaich, *Woman Plus Woman*, 1989

...We are in an intellectual climate where heterosexual writers are attended to with deference when writing about us ... but our views of heterosexuality are seen as disablingly subjective, if not tainted; a climate in which George Steiner can describe gay experience as "the damned waste land of Sodom"; where even the trendiest of prestigious critics in England, Terry Eagleton, can endorse the case for literary studies to reflect the oppression of black people and women, but say nothing whatever about homophobia; and where, if gay men's sexuality is abused, that of lesbians is utterly denied.

Mark Lilly, in the Introduction to Lilly, ed., *Lesbian and Gay Writing*, 1990

The last time people in this society cared about my rights was when I was a fetus.

Sara Cytron, quoted in *Glamour*, May 1992

They hate us. They don't want us there. And that's the way it is.

Member of ILGO, the Irish Gay and Lesbian Organization in New York City, on the homophobia of leaders and participants in the Saint Patrick's Day Parade held in New York City, on *60 Minutes*, March 14, 1993

ON PORNOGRAPHY AND LESBIANISM

Lesbians probably fascinate people more than any other sexual outsiders – except perhaps prostitutes, part of whose allure to the prurient is their reputed homosexuality ... Lesbian exhibitions are often requested in brothels, and mutual female love-making is almost obligatory in pornography.

                    Arno Karlen, *Sexuality and Homosexuality,* 1971

The lesbian [in male pornography] is colonialized, reduced to a variant of woman-as-sex-object, used to demonstrate and prove that male power pervades and invades even the private sanctuary of women with each other ... the women still sexually service the male, for whose pleasure they are called into existence.

                    Andrea Dworkin, in *Sinister Wisdom,* Fall 1980

This negative morality which pervades our society is the root not only of homophobia but of the punishing violence of much pornography. We won't move freely in the world until all people are required to confront their sexual natures in order to understand, take responsibility for and celebrate them, as we have had to.

                    Jane Rule, *A Hot-Eyed Moderate,* 1985

Lesbians are tired of having our love labeled "pornographic," while the real pornographers make money off of women's bodies ... Indeed, it is only in such pornography where men exploit lesbianism to their own ends, that the portrayal of lesbianism becomes okay to patriarchy.

                    Charlotte Bunch, *Passionate Politics,* 1987

PART V

THE MYTHICAL LESBIAN

THE MALE PARTY LINE ON LESBIANS

[P ussy] lay in the crook of Bond's arm and looked up at him. She said, not in a gangster's voice, or a lesbian's, but in a girl's voice, "Will you write to me in Sing Sing?" Bond looked down into her deep violet eyes that were no longer hard, imperious. He bent and kissed them lightly. He said, "They told me you only liked women." She said, "I never met a man before." His mouth came down ruthlessly on hers.

Ian Fleming, *Goldfinger,* 1959

"W hat makes you queer, Laura? You tell me."
"What makes you normal, Milo?"
"I was born that way. Don't tell me you were born queer! Ha!"
And he was sarcastic now.

Ann Bannon, *Women in the Shadows,* 1959

"I 'm a Lesbian."
"Oh hell, Francie, I may not be the most romantic guy in the world, but we get along all right. This is some notion you've picked up out of a book or something. Tell you what it is, women get this way when they start to get middle-aged."

Valerie Taylor, Francie and Bill, *Return to Lesbos,* 1982

ON THE MALE PARTY LINE ON LESBIANS

M en who are obsessed with sex are convinced that lesbians are obsessed with sex. Actually, like any other woman lesbians are obsessed with love and fidelity. They're also strongly interested in independence and in having a life work to do.

Judy Grahn, in *Gay Women's Liberation,* January 1970

The whole idea of homosexual experience in a man's life is so much more written about, only because women's homosexuality isn't taken seriously. Even when they do think about it, men think a woman homosexual could be turned around by a good night in bed with a man. It's not threatening, because they assume there couldn't be true love between two women.

> Gloria Steinem, quoted in Digby Diehl, *Supertalk,* 1974

Women who love women are Lesbians. Men, because they can only think of women in sexual terms, define Lesbian as sex between women.

> Rita Mae Brown, *A Plain Brown Rapper,* 1976

The male party line concerning Lesbians is that women become Lesbians out of reaction to men. This is a pathetic illustration of the male ego's inflated proportions. I became a Lesbian because of women, because women are beautiful, strong and compassionate.

> Rita Mae Brown, *A Plain Brown Rapper,* 1976

The possibility of a woman who does not exist sexually for men – the lesbian possibility – is buried, erased, occluded, distorted, misnamed, and driven underground.

> Adrienne Rich, "Compulsory Heterosexuality and Lesbian Existence," 1980, *Blood, Bread, and Poetry,* 1986

THE LESBIAN VILLAIN, VAMPIRE, AND VICTIM

"Oh, you darling," she said in a hungry whisper, "oh, you darling."

"V.V.! how did you get in? Gordon locked up hours ago."

"I had your house-key copied while you were away," said V.V. and did not wait to hear how Gillian took this announcement but strode across the room and knelt by the bedside, thrusting her long, bony arms in under the bed-clothes and dragging Gillian to the edge of the bed in an almost angry hug. Gillian struggled out of the straining clasp and sat up, pulling the ends of her long plaits from under the sheet...

> Naomi G. Royde-Smith, *The Tortoiseshell Cat,* 1925. V.V. is Victoria Vanderleyden, who preys on her young victim, Gillian. At one point in the novel V.V. tells Gillian: "You baby, I should like to eat you."

What he read caused him no particular shock – he had known of Odette's relations with Sonia before – only a faint physical revulsion. But above all he felt a sadness connected with the sight of the empty drawers, and pity for Odette, with her vacant look, her slimness and vulnerability – Odette the victim drowned in the carnivorous flower's embrace.

> Arthur Koestler, describing Peter's reaction to Odette's relationship with Sonia, *Arrival and Departure,* 1943

ON THE LESBIAN
VILLAIN, VAMPIRE, AND VICTIM

Lesbians are many times stereotyped as predatory, masculined women who prey upon young girls and seduce young women, or as sexually permissive and indiscriminate in their choice of female partners. Nothing could be further from the truth.

> Del Martin and Paul Mariah, in Herbert A. Otto, ed., *Love Today,* 1972

Lesbians are sharks, vampires, creatures from the deep lagoon, godzillas, hydrogen bombs, inventions of the laboratory, were-wolves – all of whom stalk Beverly Hills by night. Christopher Lee, in drag, in the Hammar Films middle-period, is my ideal lesbian.

> Bertha Harris, in *Sinister Wisdom,* Spring 1977

For a long time, the lesbian has been a personification of feminine evil.

> Adrienne Rich, "The Meaning of Our Love for Women Is What We Have Constantly to Expand," 1977, *On Lies, Secrets, and Silence,* 1979

Lesbians are scapegoated, by men and het women, for male crimes. Lesbians are portrayed as girl-molesters, when it's *men* who are the rapists, and when Lesbians ourselves are among the many girl victims of rape by male relatives and strangers.

> Ruston, Bev Jo, and Linda Strega, in *Lesbian Ethics,* Fall 1986

When we were doing it, [my character] was supposed to be very, very drunk. I said, "Why does she have to be very, very drunk?" I mean, if you're going to bed with a woman ... and she looks like Catherine Deneuve, and she's as charming as Catherine Deneuve, why make [my character] drunk?

> Susan Sarandon, on the lesbian vampire cult film *The Hunger,* 1991, quoted in *The Advocate,* October 6, 1992

The real irony is that lesbians are much more likely to be the victims of violence. And these homophobic portrayals cause increased violence.

> Ellen Carton, on the effect of portraying lesbians as homicidal, quoted in *Ms.,* January/February 1992

Apparently, in many minds the leap from the butch to the butcher knife is but a tiny one.

> Lindsy Van Gelder, on how lesbians are often depicted as criminals in the media, film, and academic studies, in *Ms.*, January/February 1992

OTHER MYTHS ABOUT LESBIANS

When girls are so sentimentally fond of each other that they are like silly lovers when together, and weep over each other's absence in uncontrollable agony, the conditions are serious enough for the consultation of a physician. It is an abnormal state of affairs, and if probed thoroughly might be found to be a sort of perversion, a sex mania, needing immediate and perhaps severe measures.

> Mary Wood-Allen, *What a Young Woman Ought to Know*, 1898, quoted in Jonathan Katz, *Gay/Lesbian Almanac*, 1983

When sleeping in the same bed with another girl, old or young, avoid "snuggling up" close together. Avoid the touching of sexual parts, including the breasts, and, in fact, I might say avoid contact of any parts of the body at all. Keep your night robe about you so that you are as well protected from outside contact as its size will permit, and let your conversation be of other topics than sexuality. Do not lie in each other's arms when awake or falling asleep; and, after going to bed, if you are sleeping alone or with others, just bear in mind that beds are sleeping places. When you go to bed, go to sleep just as quickly as you can.

> Irving D. Steinhardt, *Ten Sex Talks to Girls*, 1914

Courtship in Mytilene is complicated by the fact that both the principals are women. There is often, to be sure, an assumption of masculinity by one or the other or sometimes both, but it rarely survives such a searching test of courtship. Inevitably they both have to take turns at playing the maiden loth. They both have to struggle to escape. And they are both at any crisis apt to become as passive as ordinary women. Which is, if you come to think of it, a little humiliating. The mighty Sappho herself must have been aware of the fact.

Compton Mackenzie, *Extraordinary Women*, 1928

W henever masculine women were discussed, mention was made of their superior intelligence, their thirst for knowledge and their desire for culture, coupled with an abnormal tendency to spendthriftness, a passionate desire for luxury, and an unnatural predilection for beautiful foot-gear. Mention was made, too, of weird Don Juan natures who passed with insatiable lust from one adventure to another. As a result of such readings, Myra was left in the most dreadful bewilderment.

Anna Elisabet Weirauch, *The Scorpion*, 1932

W hen they still retain female garments, these women usually show traits of masculine simplicity ... disdain for the pretty feminine artifices of the toilet ... brusque, energetic movements, the attitude of the arms, the direct speech, the inflexions of the voice, the masculine straightforwardness and sense of honor, and especially the attitude toward men, free from any suggestion either of shyness or audacity.

Havelock Ellis, *Studies in the Psychology of Sex*, 1936

I t is my honest conviction that ... a female homosexual, or "lesbian," is attracted mostly, if not exclusively, to young women who are feminine inwardly as well as outwardly.

Nathaniel Thornton, *Problems in Abnormal Behavior*, 1946

People who have been greatly intimidated or have a low self-esteem ... have a tendency to cling to their own sex because it is less frightening ... the frightened woman fears to test whether she is sufficiently attractive to win a man...

Clara Thompson, in Patrick Mullahy, ed., *A Study of Interpersonal Relations,* 1949

The lesbians play first at being a man; then even being a lesbian becomes a game; masculine clothing, at first a disguise, becomes a uniform; and under the pretext of escaping male oppression, woman becomes enslaved to the character she plays; wishing not to be confined in woman's situation, she is imprisoned in that of the lesbian.

Simone de Beauvoir, *The Second Sex,* 1952

Many women who are employed in workshops and offices, surrounded by women, and who see little of men, will tend to form amorous friendships with females ... The absence or difficulty of heterosexual contacts will doom them to inversion. It is hard to draw the line between resignation and predilection: a woman can devote herself to women because man has disappointed her, but sometimes man has disappointed her because in him she was really seeking a woman.

Simone de Beauvoir, *The Second Sex,* 1952

There is seldom any permanence to a lesbian alliance.

Frank S. Caprio, *Female Homosexuality,* 1954

The lesbian is the little girl who couldn't grow up...

Ann Aldrich, *We Walk Alone,* 1955

He admitted that he wanted her. He took her in his bearish arms and kissed her mouth brutally. And Laura, in her shock, told him what she was, a Lesbian. And who had done it to her;

her own father ... His perverted love for her had twisted her whole personality.

> Ann Bannon, *Journey to a Woman,* 1960

The female homosexual may chiefly be found in the haunts of boys. She is the rival in their play, preferring the rocking-horse, playing at soldiers, etc., to dolls and other girlish occupations. The toilet is neglected, and rough boyish manners are affected. Love of art finds a substitute in the pursuits of the sciences.

> Richard von Krafft-Ebing, *Psychopathia Sexualis,* 1965

Homosexual couples often have much hostility to contend with because the partners are too close to each other. Heterosexuals have an advantage here.

> A recapitulation of the findings of psychotherapist Clarence Tripp, in *The Ladder,* March 1966

The Lesbian is an only child.

> John R. Cavanaugh, *Counseling the Invert,* 1966

...an important factor in the making of a lesbian is the girl's relationship with her father. Just as the presence of a dominant mother is often found in male homosexuality, so the absence of a satisfactory father is a frequent characteristic of female homosexuality.

> Eustace Chesser, *Strange Loves: The Human Aspects of Sexual Deviation,* 1971

Often their homosexuality is sublimated by plunging into good works ... In her efficiently run home she insists on separate beds if not separate rooms. Yet who would suspect such a pillar of respectability of unconscious homosexuality?

> Eustace Chesser, *Strange Loves: The Human Aspects of Sexual Deviation,* 1971

Biologically sex between women would be "impractical" under other than the bedroom situation. Thus, while the life of the homosexual man is often public and complicated, the life of his female counterpart can be kept private and that is often what it is.

> Marcel T. Saghir and Eli Robins, *Male and Female Homosexuality*, 1973

Lesbianism has always seemed to me an extremely inventive response to the shortage of men, but otherwise not worth the trouble.

> Nora Ephron, *Heartburn*, 1983

The sexual activities of gay males tend to be quick and genital and involve a variety of partners. Lesbians tend to engage in loving, tender, and nongenital activities with relatively permanent partners. *The vast majority of us still prefer to try to blend those two styles, and always will.*

> Kathy Keeton, *Woman of Tomorrow*, 1985

ON MYTHS ABOUT LESBIANS

Among the dire results of my "unnaturalness" I had been told that I should go blind and go mad. I believed this. In a kind of cold reasonableness, I tried to teach myself to type and play the piano with my eyes shut, against the time I should be blind.

> Valentine Ackland, in the aftermath of her parents' discovery in 1922 that she and a school friend, Lana, had been lovers. She was forbidden any further communication with Lana. *For Sylvia: An Honest Account*, 1985

I also came across odd things in the books I read. For example, I read that homosexuals could not whistle. I could whistle, so I didn't quite know what to make of that. I learned that the favorite color of homosexuals was green, and my favorite color was not green.

Barbara Gittings and Kay Lahusen, on reading about homosexuality in the 1950s, in Eric Marcus, ed., *Making History*, 1992

Eventually, if we stick closer to the truth and everyday lives of homosexuals, without sacrificing dramatic interest, perhaps we can dispense with the old bromides burdening gay society; that is, that it is a world of shadows; a world in the twilight; a world full of oversexed half-men and half-women, all blundering around in the dusk without giving a damn for anything but who they'll spend the dark hours with.

Ann Bannon, in *One: The Homosexual Viewpoint*, July 1961

Society has taught most Lesbians to believe they are sick, and has taught most straight women to despise and fear the Lesbian as a perverted, diseased creature. It has fostered the myth that Lesbians are ugly and turn to each other because they can't get that prize, that prince, a male! In this age of the new "sexual revolution," another myth has been fostered: the beautiful Lesbians who play games with each other on the screen for the titillation of heterosexual males.

Martha Shelly, 1969, in Robin Morgan, ed., *Sisterhood Is Powerful*, 1970

So little is known about the Lesbian that even Lesbians themselves are caught up in the myths and stereotypes so prevalent in our society.

Del Martin and Phyllis Lyon, *Lesbian/Woman*, 1972

Behind the liberal politeness
You're dying to know
Instead of the chat about societal attitudes
What you'd really like to ask is
Which of us in this relationship
Wears the trousers.

> Maria Jastrzebska, "Which of Us Wears the Trousers," in Christian McEwen, ed., *Naming the Waves*, 1988

That we choose to call ourselves lesbians or gay men, that we decide what this designation means to us, is itself a challenge to how same-sex loving has most often been defined in our culture. For by and large we have been the defined not the self-definers, the object of others' mythmaking rather than the creators of our own mythology.

> Christine Downing, *Myths and Mysteries of Same-Sex Love*, 1989

If homosexuality is a disease, let's all call in queer to work. "Hello, can't work today, still queer."

> Robin Tyler, at the March on Washington for Lesbian, Gay, and Bi Equal Rights, April 25, 1993

PART VI

INTERNALIZED HOMOPHOBIA AND REBELLION

THE LOVE THAT DARE NOT SPEAK ITS NAME

The loves of women for each other grow more numerous each day, and I have pondered much why these things were. That so little should be said about them surprises me, for they are everywhere...

> Frances E. Willard, *Glimpses of Fifty Years,* 1889

Whatever is felt upon the page without being specifically named there – that, one might say, is created. It is the inexplicable presence of the thing not named, of the overtone divined by the ear but not heard by it, the verbal mood, the emotional aura of the fact or the thing or the deed, that gives high quality to the novel or the drama, as well as to poetry itself.

> Willa Cather, "The Novel Démeublé," 1922. Cather, who in adolescence baptized herself William Cather, Jr., was known to her classmates at the University of Nebraska as "just plain Billy." In *Great Short Works of Willa Cather,* ed. Robert K. Miller, 1989

I remember hanging out around the bars in 1948. They were dreadful, fearful places, as were our lives. We were so scared we didn't even use our real names and certainly never used last names. There were dozens of nicknames – Tex, Mom, Boss, Brandy...

> Roberta, quoted in Sasha G. Lewis, *Sunday's Women,* 1979

There were moments when she burned with desire to draw Hilda to her side and say openly and honestly, "Dear girl – you know just as well as I that what there is between us is different from – from – from what is between other girls. But perhaps you don't know that since the creation of the world thousands of women have felt drawn towards each other like you and I ... Oh,

Hilda, I know too well that you feel the same, even if you don't say anything...

> Agnete Holk, Vita about Hilda, *Strange Friends,* 1955

P eople asked us if we were sisters
They asked us
in order to force us to lie
about our relationship
because we were constantly together
because we were lovers

> Fran Winant, "Looking at Women," *Looking at Women,* 1971

I wrote at a steady three hours a day, with Isabelle's river tresses in my mouth, in my throat ... There was more to be said, and I was unable to say it. I failed; there is no doubt in my mind about that. I don't regret my labors. It was an attempt. Other women will go on from there, others will succeed where I failed.

> Violette Leduc, of *Thérèse et Isabelle. Mad in Pursuit,* 1971

W hy can't I speak? Why can't I raise my hand and say, "I too love a woman and it's the most beautiful thing in my life?" Why can't I stop trembling? My hand threatens to fly up against my will to force the pronouncement, to force me to speak about my life with pride.

> Ruth Baetz, on a discussion about lesbianism in sociology class at U.C. Santa Barbara in 1972, in Margaret Cruikshank, ed., *The Lesbian Path,* 1985

I never said I was a dyke even to a dyke because there wasn't a dyke in the land who thought she should be a dyke or even that she was a dyke so how could we talk about it.

> Jill Johnston, *Lesbian Nation,* 1973

The word *lesbian* must be affirmed because to discard it is to collaborate with silence and lying about our very existence; with the closet-game, the creation of the *unspeakable*.

> Adrienne Rich, "It Is the Lesbian in Us...," 1976, *On Lies, Secrets, and Silence,* 1979

Between the time of Sappho and the birth of Natalie Clifford Barney (between ca. 613 B.C. and A.D. 1876) lies a "lesbian silence" of twenty-four centuries.

> Bertha Harris, in Ginny Vida, ed., *Our Right to Love,* 1978

The roots of the archives lie in the silenced voices, the love letters destroyed, the pronouns changed, the diaries carefully edited, the pictures never taken, the euphemized distortions that patriarchy would let pass.

> Joan Nestle, in the *Lesbian Herstory Archives Newsletter,* Spring 1979

Closets stand for prisons, not privacy.

> Robin Tyler, on her album *Always a Bridesmaid Never a Groom,* 1979

We have been silent for too long; we have been silenced for too long. For the first time in centuries, we can now hear the music of other Lesbian voices.

> Julia Penelope Stanley and Susan J. Wolfe, in Stanley and Wolfe, eds., *The Coming Out Stories,* 1980

Being queer is like being on a lifetime assignment as a secret agent in some foreign country. No matter how careful you are, no matter how practiced you are at simulating the natives, you know at any minute you may be uncovered.

> Noretta Koertge, *Who Was That Masked Woman?,* 1981

One may identify as a lesbian, but lesbianism has little re-claimed history and no traditions. There are no celebrations to mark the stages in the life of a lesbian, her initiation or her union with another, no coming-of-age rituals, weddings, or lesbian gatherings at the birth of a child. Even at her death, a lesbian's life-long commitment to another woman may be contested or made invisible by omission.

> Savine Teubal, 1982, quoted in Amy Appleby, ed., *Quentin Crisp's Book of Quotations,* 1989

"Does this mean you always were?"

"What?"

"A lesbian."

Folly realized it was easier for Mary Lou to say that word than for her. She felt a stranger to it and a recognition at the same time.

> Maureen Brady, *Folly,* 1982

Everytime we heard,
"I don't mind gays
but why must they
be blatant?" and said nothing—
It was an act of perversion.

> Pat Parker, "Where Will You Be?," in Barbara Smith, ed., *Home Girls,* 1983

We're invisible, we're like stealth lesbians, low-flying and un-detectable.

> Kate Clinton, quoted in *The Advocate,* December 17, 1991

I had discovered spelunking at the library when I stopped in to see what they had about lesbians. I found a book called *Lesbian/Woman,* but I was frightened to be seen reading it, so I wrapped it in a *Life* magazine.

> Wendy Caster, "Spelunking," in Karen Barber, ed., *Bushfire,* 1991

...there are a lot of major voices in the lesbian community that will not speak their names, and there's nothing we can do about that.

> Lanford Wilson, in an interview in *The Advocate,* April 20, 1993

CONFORMITY

They accept, with heads bowed – angry, hurt, and helpless – and often with some sense that perhaps their lot is not entirely without justification ... the worst effect of discrimination has been to make homosexuals doubt themselves and share in the general contempt for sexual inverts.

> Donald W. Cory, *The Homosexual in America,* 1951

Lesbians tend to conform mightily in the hope, however futile that if they are all upright and uptight, somehow they will be allowed to continue their second-class existence forever.

> Gene Damon (pseudonym of Barbara Grier), in Robin Morgan, ed., *Sisterhood Is Powerful,* 1970

Another common denominator of my self-labeled lesbian patients is that often they are so glad to be tolerated that they accept even more abuse than non-lesbian women.

> Jean Mundy, in the *Homosexual Counseling Journal,* October 1974

Visibility is important, psychologically, because of the profound role played by its opposite in the life of every homosexual – that is, secretiveness.

> Paul Robinson, in the *New Republic,* June 3, 1978

Overcompensation is a trap that lesbians and gays, like members of other devalued minorities, may fall into. Hoping to earn the respect of those who reject our lifestyles, and attain some precious job security, we may work harder and longer than our heterosexual coworkers.

Marny Hall, *The Lavender Couch,* 1985

We are all in retreat, trying to merge with the wallpaper, get jobs, say nothing. Danger distracts one from abstract thought.

Anna Wilson, in Lesley Saunders, ed., *Glancing Fires,* 1987

If I had to wear high heels and a dress, I would be a mental case.

k.d. lang, 1992, quoted in *The Advocate,* October 6, 1992

SELF-LOATHING

Sometimes I've caught myself dwelling on the thought of some woman, I've stamped my foot in anger & tried to turn my mind toward other things, for I realize the danger of going to an extreme.

Martha Lavell, from a diary entry, May 1, 1930, quoted in Penelope Franklin, ed., *Private Pages,* 1986

Later, wrapped in Nicoli's close embrace in the silken blackness of her bedroom, Sheila found a love that was forever to set her apart from the world and bind her always to that world of shadow and shade whence there is no escape.

Lilyan Brock, *Queer Patterns,* 1935

That night she stared at herself in the glass; and even as she did so, she hated her body with its muscular shoulders, its small compact breasts, and its slender flanks of an athlete. All her life she must drag this body of hers like a monstrous fetter imposed on her spirit. This strangely ardent yet sterile body ... She longed to maim it...

> Radclyffe Hall, describing Stephen's hatred of her body, *The Well of Loneliness,* 1949

"You're scared to admit what you really are, and more afraid to admit that you could be in love with me. Is being gay such a terrible thing? Do you think you'll turn purple, or grow an extra head?"

> Paula Christian, Toni to Val, *Edge of Twilight,* 1959

"You were giving me *yourself,*" she said. "Can't you see that, Jo? Gordon was some kind of vehicle you used to get *yourself* across to *me.*"

"You're out of your mind."

"Am I? Tell me honestly, Jo: have you ever heard of a woman who could make love with a man as rapturously, as completely as you said you did with Gordon and then, three minutes after it was all over, dash to a typewriter and send it all to some girl she knew?..."

> Marjorie Lee, Frannie and Jo, *The Lion House,* 1959

Perhaps a relationship between two women must always be incomplete – unless, I suppose, they have Lesbian inclinations which I don't happen to share. Then, or so I have been given to understand, the concord may approach perfection. You see, there is a kind of free-masonry between women – and no doubt between men also — which makes up for the more elemental excitement of the sex-war.

> Vita Sackville-West, expressing Laura's opinion of lesbian love. She then states that jealousy is a serious "snag" in lesbian relationships. *No Signpost in the Sea,* 1961

She is a jewish/catholic 38-year-old reformed-alcoholic dyke who thinks that being a lesbian is the worst misfortune in the world. She is a small sad cocky individual permanently barred from the respect of her fellow citizens, whose only satisfying relationship is with her poodle, Anna Pavlova.

> Sandra Boucher, "Mountain Radio," quoted in *Sinister Wisdom,* Fall 1976

"And we're just a couple of dykes." She spit the words into the air. Lorraine started as if she'd been slapped. "That's a filthy thing to say, Tee..."

> Gloria Naylor, Theresa and Lorraine, *The Women of Brewster Place,* 1980

I'm not a Lesbian. Lesbians. Lez-bee-yuns. Les beans.

> Joanna Russ, *On Strike against God,* 1980

"I tried to be what you'd like — a woman who liked men. I lay low as long as I could, and then I couldn't any longer. My God, I was walking around with a belly full of hot coals, thinking about you. I think about you all day and dream about you all night. I thought, I've got to tell her, and if she despises me for it it can't be any worse."

> Margaret Creal, Ariadne to Andrea, "Two Women," *The Man Who Sold Prayers,* 1981

ON SELF-LOATHING

The dread of homosexuality is a result of, and derives its tremendous force from, the wishes for homosexual expression which are present in our unconscious minds. In other words the fear is intimately connected with the wish, and the wish is only repressed because of the dread which is conjured up by the social taboo.

>　Martin Hoffman, *The Gay World: Homosexuality and the Social Creation of Evil,* 1968

Saddest of all, there are those who know their homosexual leanings and reject them as unclean and unfit. They are victims of what must be the best and the longest advertising campaign in history, simply that homosexuality is perverted, wrong, bad, evil, despicable, and every other loaded word you can conceive of.

>　Gene Damon (pseudonym of Barbara Grier), in Robin Morgan, ed., *Sisterhood Is Powerful,* 1970

Lesbians and homosexuals all seek love ... Some have become so alienated from people because of society's strictures that they have lost touch with their worth and dignity as human beings and cannot love themselves, cannot accept themselves. Their values so negated, they lose the desire to live, because their desire to love has been forever thwarted.

>　Del Martin and Paul Mariah, in Herbert A. Otto, ed., *Love Today,* 1972

We have been taught to hate ourselves and how thoroughly we have learned the lesson.

>　Andrew Hodges and David Hutter, *With Downcast Gays,* 1977

Fear of the label "lesbian" has driven many into matrimony, mental hospitals, and – worst of all – numbing, dumbing normal-ity. It has driven others into heterosexist "gay pride" protests promoted by and for men, into butch-femme matings modeled on matrimony, into aping the genital fixations of porn peddlers, pimps, priests.

Mary Daly, *Gyn/Ecology*, 1978

Some homosexuals, because of societal proscription, have developed such phobic reactions ... that they believe themselves transsexuals and would rather give up their gender than face a life of homosexual behavior.

T. Shtasel, 1979, quoted in Leslie Martin Lothstein, *Female-to-Male Transsexualism*, 1983

The truly gay person must root out internalized homophobia ... By a process of ruthless Augustinian introspection, one must examine one's soul for remnants of guilt, shame, self-hate and fear, and perform the necessary excisions.

John P. de Cecco, in the *Journal of Homosexuality*, Summer 1981

There have always been some who have been gay and proud; but for every Natalie Barney, there have been many more Radclyffe Halls, accepting the degrading descriptions of psychologists, inevitable suffering, and a need for pity.

Jane Rule, "Closet-Burning," *Outlander*, 1981

Of course it is extremely difficult to like oneself in a culture which thinks you are a disease.

Chrystos, in Cherríe Moraga and Gloria Anzaldúa, eds., *This Bridge Called My Back*, 1983

Our sexuality is such a deep, spontaneous, and powerful part of our core identity that the conscious need to falsify it is a little death.

Gloria Steinem, *Revolution from Within*, 1992

BREAKING THE BONDS OF PATRIARCHY

Comin' a time, BD women, they ain't goin' to need no men. Oh, the way they treat us is a low down and dirty thing.

> Bessie Jackson, from the song "BD [bulldyker] Women's Blues," 1935, reissued on the album *AC-DC Blues: Gay Jazz Reissues*

Lesbianism is one road to freedom — freedom from oppression by men.

> Martha Shelly, 1969, in Robin Morgan, ed., *Sisterhood Is Powerful,* 1970

Whatever their physical type, educational level, temperament or mentality, all homosexual women are *one* in their rejection of bondage to the male.

> Charlotte Wolff, *Love between Women,* 1971

I wished I could walk down the streets and not hear those constant, abrasive sounds from the mouths of the opposite sex. Damn, I wished the world would let me be myself.

> Rita Mae Brown, *Rubyfruit Jungle,* 1973

My music doesn't work when men are present.

> Alix Dobkin, quoted in the *Lesbian Tide,* November/December 1974

We ought never be taught to read. We fight through the constant male refractoriness of our surroundings; our souls are torn out of us with such shock that there isn't even any blood. Remember: I didn't and don't want to be a "feminine" version or a diluted version or a special version or a subsidiary version or an ancillary version, or an adapted version of the heroes I admire. I want to be the heroes themselves.

> Joanna Russ, *The Female Man,* 1975

Our very strength as lesbians lies in the fact that we are outside of patriarchy; our existence challenges its life.

> Charlotte Bunch, in *Quest 2*, 1975

The experience of maternity and the experience of sexuality have both been channeled to serve male interests; behavior which threatens the institutions, such as illegitimacy, abortion, lesbianism, is considered deviant or criminal.

> Adrienne Rich, *Of Woman Born*, 1976

...Being a womon-identified-womon, a lesbian, is: opposing the male sex and everything it represents, realistically, and opposing the masculinization of the female sex.

> Mia Albright, in *Sinister Wisdom*, Spring 1977

Every lesbian personality I have knowledge of is in some way creative. To my mind this is because she is freed or has freed herself from the external and internal dominance of the male...

> Elsa Gidlow, in *Heresies*, May 1977

The lesbian is most clearly the antithesis of patriarchy – an offense to its basic tenets: It is woman-hating; we are woman-loving. It demands female obedience and docility; we seek strength, assertiveness, and dignity for women.

> Charlotte Bunch, in Ginny Vida, ed., *Our Right to Love*, 1978

Lesbianism is a threat to the ideological, political, personal, and economic basis of male supremacy. The Lesbian threatens the ideology of male supremacy by destroying the lie about female inferiority, weakness, passivity, and by denying women's "innate" need for men. Lesbians literally do not need men...

> Charlotte Bunch, in Alison M. Jaggar and Paula Rothenberg Struhl, eds., *Feminist Frameworks*, 1978

The woman-identified-woman commits herself to other women for political, emotional, physical, and economic support. Women are important to her. She is important to herself. Our society demands that commitment from women be reserved for men.

> Charlotte Bunch, in Alison M. Jaggar and Paula Rothenberg Struhl, eds., *Feminist Frameworks*, 1978

...lesbian women, who are neither economically nor sexually dependent on men, may be described as the least conforming category of women and thus may be expected to evidence higher levels of psychological adjustment, self-esteem, and occupational achievement than nonlesbian women.

> Virginia R. Brooks, *Minority Stress and Lesbian Women*, 1981

If men really are turned on by all that awful underwear, leg and footwear, all that paint and headachy perfume, then maybe they should have been wearing it all along ... If what men want is our underwear, let them be welcome to it. It's a great swap for the shirts off their backs which we wear so comfortably.

> Jane Rule, *A Hot-Eyed Moderate*, 1985

The society of male bonding may peer at the lesbian from afar, but the possibility of the friends' existence defies and defiles its principles of logic. The male-defined principle of identity and its correlates, the principle of difference and the principle of equality, cannot think the lesbian.

> Jeffner Allen, *Lesbian Philosophy*, 1986

I break with reproductive memory. I no longer claim to be wo-man, the counterpart of man, she who is possessed by men. *I posit my own freedom. I place myself with all who will be women no longer: lesbians.*

> Jeffner Allen, *Lesbian Philosophy*, 1986

Men reflect women *half* their natural size.
Dell Richards, *Lesbian Lists,* 1990

A lesbian is defying the most sacred traditional female role of male partner, and she pays for it.
Paula Kamen, *Feminist Fatale,* 1991

Lesbian women often fear ridicule, if not physical attack, both from men they know and from anonymous men in public.
Ellyn Kaschak, *Engendered Lives,* 1992

LESBIAN-FEMINIST ACTIVISM

If you do not want to hear the truth about things which have been greeted with the most dangerous weapon, "S-s-s-sh," don't read this book, said weapon being in my mind more dangerous to the development of the human mind and soul than the machine gun is to the body of a man placed in front of the firing line.
Mary Casal, on the dangers of a lack of dialogue about sexuality and homosexuality, *The Stone Wall,* 1930

In Anglo-Saxon countries it seems ... that female homosexuality means rather more than Sapphic lyricism, since it somehow acts as a stimulus to the social and political organization of women...
Carl Jung, "The Love Problem of a Student," 1922, in *Civilization in Transition, The Collected Works of Carl Jung,* trans. R.F.C. Hull, 1964

Homosexuals should be judged as individuals
Message on a sign held by Barbara Gittings at a rally in Philadelphia, July 4, 1965

First Class Citizenship for Homosexuals.

> Message on a sign held by a marcher at a White House demonstration sponsored by the Mattachine Society of Washington, 1965

As homosexuals we share the dubious honor with males of being "the last of the minority groups." As Lesbians we are even lower in the sand hole; we are women (itself a majority/minority status) and we are Lesbians: the last half of the least noticed, most disadvantaged minority. There is no room here for any other cause. We have the biggest bag to carry and we need a good many strong shoulders. Get your head out of the sand hole and help with this very urgent, very needful battle.

> Marilyn Barrow (pseudonym of Barbara Grier), "The Least of These," in *The Ladder,* 1968

Fortunately, Lesbianism never really had anything to do with men, despite all attempts at interference, and as a consequence remains the only viable pursuit left on earth as pure as snow, ego-free, and non-profit.

> Susan Helenius, July 9, 1971, quoted in Alice Echols, *Daring to Be Bad,* 1989

To say that the homosexual *by definition* cannot love is the Big Lie, a gigantic hoax compounded for too many centuries.

> Del Martin and Paul Mariah, in Herbert A. Otto, ed., *Love Today,* 1972

If you want high consciousness, I'll tell you what to do,
You got to talk to a woman, let her talk to you.
You got to build you a union and make it strong,
And if we stick together, girls, it won't be long...
Of course, it ain't that simple, so I'd better explain...
You got to ride on the lesbian train...

> Alix Dobkin, from the song "Talking Lesbian," on the album *Lavender Jane Loves Women,* 1974

Heterosexism can be cured.

> Public service message from the Oscar Wilde Bookshop, in *Christopher Street,* March 1977

Before any kind of feminist movement existed, or could exist, lesbians existed: women who loved women, who refused to comply with the behavior demanded of women, who refused to define themselves in relation to men.

> Adrienne Rich, "The Meaning of Our Love for Women Is What We Have Constantly to Expand," 1977, *On Lies, Secrets, and Silence,* 1979

The gay movement is the avant-garde of the new quest for self-awareness, and if it should perish, we, the heterosexual "inner émigrés," won't have flanks anymore.

> Jerzy Kosinski, 1978, quoted in *The Advocate,* October 6, 1992

A Lesbian feminist, Sally,
Was attacked by a man in an alley.
Having studied karate,
She clobbered him dotty,
And went to her women's rights rally.

> Eleanor Smith, limerick in the First Annual Lesbian-Feminist Limerick Contest, in *Albatross,* Winter 1978

It is time to recognize that lesbians and homosexuals are individuals like anyone else, who happen to have made certain personal choices about their private lives ... They are fully entitled to the same Constitutional protection as all other Americans.

> Bella Abzug, in Ginny Vida, ed., *Our Right to Love,* 1978

All the women leaned each on others, yet nowhere was there a burden – closely fitting, closely entwined, Artilidea at the center held by all.

> Sally Gearhart, *The Wanderground,* 1979

You are a special woman, shouldn't have to hide.
I want to know you, grow with you right by my side.
Won't you come as you are, won't you do what you must,
Won't you help build a sisterhood we all can trust?

> Betsy Ross, from the song "Don't Shut My Sister Out," on the album *Sweet Sorcery* (with Cathy Winter), 1980

Why should we be "embarrassed" by the alleged affair between Eleanor Roosevelt and Lorena Hickok?... Does it sweep away even one of Mrs. Roosevelt's considerable achievements? Does it alter one iota that fact of her decency, morality and humanity? It does not. They are as valid as when we all believed that she was perfectly heterosexual. It should not tarnish our opinion of Mrs. Roosevelt. It should raise our consciousness about homosexuality.

> C.S. Barnes, in response to a *New York Post* article by Harriet Van Horne condemning Eleanor Roosevelt for revealing her lesbianism. Quoted in Bernice Goodman, *"Where Will You Be?" The Professional Oppression of Gay People,* 1980

For a woman to be a lesbian in a male-supremacist, capitalist, misogynist, racist, homophobic, imperialist culture, such as that of North America, is an act of resistance.

> Cheryl Clarke, in Cherríe Moraga and Gloria Anzaldúa, eds., *This Bridge Called My Back,* 1981

Those of us who stand outside the circle of this society's definition of acceptable women; those of us who have been forged in the crucibles of difference; those of us who are poor, who are lesbians, who are black, who are older, know that *survival is not an academic skill.* It is learning how to stand alone, unpopular and sometimes reviled, and how to make common cause with those others identified as outside the structures, in order to define and seek a world in which we can all flourish. It is learning how to take our differences and make them strengths. *For the master's tools will never dismantle the master's house.*

> Audre Lorde, in Cherríe Moraga and Gloria Anzaldúa, eds., *This Bridge Called My Back,* 1981

And as for the alleged "laws of nature," what about those lesbian seagulls on Catalina Island, off the coast of California? Or the fact that homosexuality and lesbianism existed among cats, dogs, primates, and other creatures?

> Paula Christian, *The Cruise,* 1982

Without a visual identity, we have no community, no support network, no movement. Making ourselves visible is a political act, making ourselves visible is a continual process.

> Joan E. Biren, in *Visual Communication,* Spring 1983

From Stonewall to Soweto, the people are resisting.

> Chant during the New York Lesbian and Gay Pride March, June 29, 1986

If we can raise our own hens, or buy eggs from Lesbian wimmin who raise their own hens, and mix them with mayonnaise that we make ourselves, we are one step closer to freedom.

> Bode Noonan, *Red Beans and Rice,* 1986

Who can imagine, their mind half closed down, what a lesbian might be like in a non-hostile environment – we know as little about it as we know of the effect on plants of the absence of gravity.

> Anna Wilson, in Lesley Saunders, ed., *Glancing Fires,* 1987

...**W**e know that as long as the word lesbian can strike fear in any woman's heart, then work on behalf of women can be stopped; the only successful work against sexism must include work against homophobia.

> Suzanne Pharr, *Homophobia,* 1988

Gay and lesbian overeaters have formed: Food Equals Death, or FED-UP. Inexperienced lesbian mothers with uncooperative turkey-baster babies are fighting back with: Single Parents In Trouble, or SPIT-UP. And finally, everybody with some kind of neurotic problem ... seems to be joining: Let Overwhelming Obsessions Suddenly End Now, or LOOSEN-UP.

> ACT-UP clones listed in *OutWeek,* quoted in *Outlines,* October 1989

In one sense, the vast majority of women, whether heterosexual or lesbian, have no choice but to struggle with individual men for women's and sexual liberation, since we must continue to relate to men in personal ways (as employers, relatives, politicians, etc.) whether or not we choose them as lovers.

> Ann Ferguson, *Blood at the Root,* 1989

We are so unidentifiable
such an inconvenient minority, and you have no way
of knowing
if one of us wrote that book your daughter is reading
on law, or lice, or loving.

> Jan Sellers, "Lesbians in Books," in Elaine Hobby and Chris White, eds., *What Lesbians Do in Books,* 1991

In our culture, power belongs to those who are famous. I want to be as famous, [i.e.] powerful, as possible. My gift to becoming famous is my comedy. I always knew what I wanted, I just didn't know for a long time how I was going to get it. I worry about the world, about wars, about feeding all the people who are hungry, about AIDS, about discrimination on all levels, and I want my fame to be able to help change things.

> Suzanne Westenhoefer, quoted in *Sappho's Isle,* March 1993

It's My Right To Cuddle Who I Want To Cuddle

> Message on a sign at the March on Washington for Lesbian, Gay, and Bi Equal Rights, April 25, 1993

We're coming home. So listen to us, America, our divided country, our country with too little hope. Look at these faces, look at our diversity, look at our unity. America, if we could find hope and optimism, anybody can. America, we're coming home. We're coming home to help bring this country together, to make it whole again.

> Torie Osborn, in a speech at the March on Washington for Lesbian, Gay, and Bi Equal Rights, April 25, 1993

The next time someone says to you, "You *choose* to be a lesbian, you *choose* to be a gay man," say: "No, no, no. I did not choose it. I was chosen. Yeah, stood in line, got my ticket, scratched it right off. I won!"

> Suzanne Westenhoefer, at the March on Washington for Lesbian, Gay, and Bi Equal Rights, April 25, 1993

America, this day marks the return from exile of the gay and lesbian people. We are banished no more. We wander the wilderness of despair no more. We are afraid no more.

> Urvashi Vaid, in a speech at the March on Washington for Lesbian, Gay, and Bi Equal Rights, April 25, 1993

Homophobia is a social disease

> Message on a bumper sticker seen at the Lambda
> Rising bookstore in Washington, D.C., 1993

SEPARATISM

I do not want to be separate from any women ... [but] until heterosexual women treat Lesbians as full human beings and fight the enormity of male supremacy with us, I have no option but to be separate from them just as they have no option but to be separate from men until men begin to change their own sexism.

> Rita Mae Brown, *A Plain Brown Rapper,* 1976

At this time when fascism and the New Right are on the rise, it is becoming more and more dangerous to be an open lesbian. And separatists are the most out lesbians of all.

> Bev Jo, 1981, in Sarah L. Hoagland and Julia Pene-
> lope, eds., *For Lesbians Only,* 1988

Separatism is focusing on each other as lesbians and minimizing the energy given to males.

> Anna Lee, in Jeffner Allen, ed., *Lesbian Philoso-
> phies and Cultures,* 1990

I don't understand separatism, people who live in enclaves and groups by themselves.

> Liz Smith, in an interview in *OutWeek,* June 26,
> 1991

LESBIAN HERSTORY

Steeped as we are, in an age and atmosphere of more and more learning in more and more fields, it is astonishing that so little accurate material is written about Lesbians.

> Gene Damon (pseudonym of Barbara Grier), in Robin Morgan, ed., *Sisterhood Is Powerful*, 1970

The Lesbian is one of the least known members of our culture. Less is known about her – and less accurately – than about the Newfoundland dog.

> Sidney Abbott and Barbara Love, *Sappho Was a Right-on Woman*, 1972

The Lesbian Herstory Archives exists to gather and preserve records of Lesbian lives and activities so that future generations of Lesbians will have ready access to materials relevant to their lives.

> Statement of Purpose of the Lesbian Herstory Archives in New York, in the *Lesbian Herstory Archives Newsletter* 1, June 1975

For, concerning the specificity of the desire between women, nothing has been revealed, nothing has been enunciated.

> Luce Irigaray, quoted in George Stambolian and Elaine Marks, eds., *Homosexualities and French Literature*, 1979

If any women wrote lesbian sex literature during the sixteenth to eighteenth centuries, it has been lost to posterity.

> Lillian Faderman, *Surpassing the Love of Men,* 1981

...It's a matter of time before [gay and lesbian history] is recognized as a field, and people will begin to write their theses in it ... There's a down side to that. The real texture and richness of gay and lesbian life could be lost once it's churned through the academic mill. Hopefully, because gays and lesbians will be doing that scholarship themselves, they'll be sensitive to that danger.

> Martin Duberman, in an interview in *OutWeek*, May 22, 1991

We are the only untold story.

> Carole DeSanti, quoted in *New York*, May 10, 1993

A GLIMPSE AROUND THE GLOBE

CHINA

Because homosexual desire leads to non-marriage, it is truly an offense against heaven. It is very harmful to women's health and strength ... Women passing time unmarried sink to homosexuality. Since it is extremely widespread, this is truly a great problem.

> Chen Dongyuan, ed., *History of Chinese Female Life*, 1937, quoted in Bret Hinsch, *Passions of the Cut Sleeve*, 1990

CUBA

As Gay, Lesbian and Straight Cuban Exiles, we have felt the horrors that have been perpetrated in our beloved homeland for over thirty-two years. Among all these crimes, perhaps the most horrible has been the regime's persecution of Gays and Lesbians...

> In a leaflet circulated by the Gay and Lesbian Association of Cuban Exiles at the New York Lesbian and Gay Pride March, June 30, 1991

GERMANY

From the lesbian oasis that it was, Berlin has become a sad city. Since the fall of the Wall, all the energy that had been concentrated here because of the isolation started running away, flowing out, dispersing. And I see lesbians getting more and more upright, respectable, and nice. I can't stand seeing lesbians repress themselves.

> Mahide, host of the German lesbian program *Läsbisch TV,* quoted in *The Advocate,* December 1, 1992

HONG KONG

Lady Precious Yin and Mistress White Jade lay on top of each other, their legs entwined so that their jade gates (genitalia) pressed together. They then moved in a rubbing and jerking fashion against each other like fishes gobbling flies or water plants from the surface. As they became more excited ... Great Lord Yang thrusts between them with his jade root (penis). They moved in unison until all three shared the ultimate simultaneously.

> F. Lieh-Mak, K.M. O'Hoy, and S.L. Luk, from a traditional handbook on marital intercourse (Hong Kong), in *Archives of Sexual Behavior* 12(1), 1983, quoted in Bret Hinsch, *Passions of the Cut Sleeve,* 1990

RUSSIA

Homosexuals should be shot because they are defective.

A Russian laboratory assistant, 21 years old, quoted in Adrian Gaiges and Tatiana Suvorova, *Love Outside the Plan* (in Russian and German), 1990

To the Soviet citizen, "homosexual" is as much a curse word as "prostitute," the only difference being that homosexuals are more misunderstood and more hated. It is no secret that Soviet society is misogynist ... I think that the most important thing today is for [lesbians] to come out of the underground and speak out about our problems and rights. We invite all women to respond...

Anna Vetrova, in the premier issue of *Tema*, the first gay and lesbian newspaper published in the former USSR, 1990

PROGRESS

Only recently regarded as marginal or too risky, gay and lesbian studies have moved from the sidelines to the center of academic publishing. One major reason is the simple economic fact that gay and lesbian books sell, among both academics and non-academics.

Liz McMillen, in the *Chronicle of Higher Education*, July 22, 1992

For the first time in a presidential election, gay men and lesbians are becoming major players.

New York Times, October 11, 1992

While we have always been politically active, our power as a voting bloc has been recognized only recently. We have made progress, but we still have a long way to go. Although most Americans oppose job discrimination on the basis of sexual orientation, less than a majority find homosexuality to be an acceptable "life style."

> Ellen Carton, in a Letter to the Editor, *New York Times Magazine,* October 11, 1992

We finally have a president who can at least say the words — gay and lesbian.

> Susan Anderson, on Bill Clinton winning the presidency, quoted in the *New York Times,* November 8, 1992

We're like the Evian water of the '90s. Everybody wants to know a lesbian or to be with a lesbian or just to dress like one.

> Suzanne Westenhoefer, on lesbian clout in the 1990s, quoted in *Newsweek,* June 21, 1993

Sometimes I think it's the year of the woman squared. It's sort of like the year of the woman loving woman.

> Kate Clinton, on the gains lesbians made in 1993, quoted in *Newsweek,* June 21, 1993

THE FUTURE

When the world changes and one day women are capable of seizing power and devoting themselves to the exercise of arms and letters in which they will doubtless soon excel, woe betide us.

> Monique Wittig, *Les guérillères,* 1969

I believe that if the world (if the human race) is to survive, then Lesbians will lead the way.

> Barbara Grier, in *Sinister Wisdom,* Spring 1977

Stonewall is not just about yesterday; for us it must also be about tomorrow.

> Virginia M. Apuzzo, in *Out/Look,* Summer 1989

For the foreseeable future ... gay people will remain an autonomous group with a keen sense of their social difference. Even if they want assimilation, which many do not, lingering prejudice in the dominant culture will make identification with the gay subculture inevitable.

> Margaret Cruikshank, *The Gay and Lesbian Liberation Movement,* 1992

IN SUPPORT OF LESBIANS

Homosexuality and lesbianism were very fashionable in those days. And it was quite acceptable. At least as far as I was concerned ... in those days people were always having love affairs with their poodles and putting tiny flowers in strange places. But they talked amusingly about their affairs. My family didn't though. They would have gone absolutely mad with horror.

> Alice Roosevelt Longworth, on lesbianism in the era when her father, Teddy Roosevelt, was president. In a *Washington Post* interview, quoted in *The Advocate,* March 27, 1974

It's all right for anybody to be who they are, just as long as they don't let their dogs shit in the street.

> Bette Midler, 1975, quoted in *The Advocate,* October 6, 1992

I don't see homosexuality as a threat to the family.

> Jimmy Carter, quoted in the *Washington Post*, June 19, 1977

Love is love. We're told little boys should love little girls and little girls should love little boys. We know it's not so.

> Julie Harris, 1977, quoted in *The Advocate*, October 6, 1992

I know lots of people who are gay. It's natural to me. I never know who is and who ain't anymore — especially in California.

> Dolly Parton, 1977, quoted in *The Advocate*, October 6, 1992

It's appalling that there have to be movements organized to give human beings the right to be human beings in the eyes of other human beings.

> Glenda Jackson, 1979, quoted in *The Advocate*, October 6, 1992

My attitude toward anybody's sexual persuasion is this: without deviation from the norm, progress is not possible.

> Frank Zappa, 1980, quoted in Leigh W. Rutledge, ed., *Unnatural Quotations*, 1988

It's perfectly all right with me. Some of the most gifted people I've ever met or read about are homosexual. How can you knock it?

> Lucille Ball, February 11, 1980, quoted in Leigh W. Rutledge, *The Gay Decades*, 1992

Please have a sense of humor about yourself. Especially if you're into women's lib. Shave your legs. Gay lib — do the same.

> Joan Rivers, 1983, quoted in *The Advocate*, October 6, 1992

I don't think homosexuality is a choice. Society forces you to think it's a choice, but in fact, it's in one's nature. The choice is whether one expresses one's nature truthfully or spends the rest of one's life lying about it.

> Marlo Thomas, 1985, quoted in *The Advocate,* October 6, 1992

I've known gay and lesbian people all my life ... Some of my most brilliant teachers and some of my classmates were gay. They were just a part of the community of people. I think that is what is important to understand.

> Jesse Jackson, 1988, quoted in *The Advocate,* October 6, 1992

If my kid comes to me and says "I'm gay," I'd just say, "That's fine." If my daughter says "I'm a lesbian," I'd say, "That's fine too."

> Dustin Hoffman, in an interview with London's *Daily Mail,* quoted in *Outlines,* October 1989

I have nothing against gays or lesbians. I have lots of gay boys working for me. I got a letter from the lesbians and gay association. They are going to boycott me because I said there are lesbians in jail. How do I know who's in jail? Imagine a women's jail. There must be lesbians. Maybe I should become a lesbian. What do I know? I like men.

> Zsa Zsa Gabor, in response to the uproar over her comment to reporters on the steps of the Beverly Hills courthouse when she was being tried for slapping a police officer. She said that she did not want to go to prison because "they are all lesbians in jail. And I'm so scared of lesbians." Associated Press, quoted in *Outlines,* December 1989

There's nothing wrong with going to bed with somebody of your own sex. People should be very free with sex – they should draw the line at goats.

> Elton John, quoted in William Cole and Louis Phillips, eds., *Sex: "The Most Fun You Can Have without Laughing" and Other Quotations,* 1990

I just think you're born gay. I don't think it's unnatural. Some are and some ain't. But I understand the pain of coming out.

> Roseanne Arnold, 1991, quoted in *The Advocate,* October 6, 1992

It's as if I've always known that there was nothing wrong with gay and lesbian people, that this is the natural way of life for them ... It's in the genes, and I don't think environment has a heck of a lot to do with it. I just knew that they deserved compassion and understanding.

> Abigail Van Buren, in Eric Marcus, ed., *Making History,* 1992

These are lesbian ladies ... Live as you please. And God bless you!

> Jackie Mason, in support of a lesbian couple on *The Jackie Mason Show,* November 2, 1992

When people are homophobic, I don't know what they are talking about. But then again, I'm always shocked when someone is anti-Semitic.

> Joan Rivers, in an interview in *The Advocate,* December 1, 1992

If that law were passed against Jews or people of color, the whole country would be outraged and nobody would question a boycott of that state.

> Barbra Streisand, in support of the boycott of Colorado following the passage of Amendment 2, a measure that bars legislation protecting gay men and lesbians from discrimination. Quoted in the *New York Times,* December 14, 1992

Elijah thinks Chastity is a weirdo. I've tried to explain to him that love between two women can be just as meaningful as love between a man and a woman.

> Cher, quoted in the *National Enquirer,* 1992

The Irish, the Rabbi, the Priest, the Sheik,
The Gay, the Straight, the Preacher,
The privileged, the homeless, the Teacher.
They hear. They all hear
The speaking of the Tree.

> Maya Angelou, "On the Pulse of Morning," read at President Clinton's inauguration, January 20, 1993.

I'd be fine. A lot of people I know who are gay have even gone to my mom before going to their own moms. We're very open-minded in our family...

> Debbie Gibson, in answer to the question of whether it would be okay if her child were gay, in an interview in *The Advocate,* February 23, 1993

Without homosexuals there'd be no Hollywood.

> Elizabeth Taylor, in an interview on the TV show *Larry King Live,* March 6, 1993

I don't want kids today to go through this kind of homophobia and I want to do something about it.

> Phil Donahue, on the TV show *Talk Back America,*
> March 8, 1993

We want to ideally work for a society where there will be no closet.

> Phil Donahue, on the TV show *Pozner-Donahue,*
> April 8, 1993

I'm for tolerance. Who am I? I'm not God's policeman here on earth ... I'm for civil rights.

> Elie Wiesel, on whether Jewish gay men and lesbians should be allowed to march under their own banner in the Salute to Israel Parade in New York. On NBC New York local news, April 24, 1993

I believe in an America that does not discriminate because of sexual orientation.

> David Dinkins, in a speech at the March on Washington for Lesbian, Gay, and Bi Equal Rights, April 25, 1993

I pray for the day that we all share equal rights as human beings.

> Lorna Luft, at the March on Washington for Lesbian, Gay, and Bi Equal Rights, April 25, 1993

The first person I told that I was marching was my father. He said to me, "But, Cybill, they might think you're one!" And I said, "Who cares."

> Cybill Shepherd, on her decision to participate in the March on Washington, in a speech at the March on Washington for Lesbian, Gay, and Bi Equal Rights, April 25, 1993

Our whole nation should know by now that it's not the gender of a person you love that matters, it's the quality of the love between you.

> Cybill Shepherd, in a speech at the March on Washington for Lesbian, Gay, and Bi Equal Rights, April 25, 1993

Your rights come as an American. We should not let state by state play with your rights. You should not have to be nomads, moving around, looking for wherever you can move to live openly and freely. That is your birthright.

> Patricia Schroeder, in a speech at the March on Washington for Lesbian, Gay, and Bi Equal Rights, April 25, 1993

PART VII

OUR LIVES

MOTHERS

Afraid of losing you

I ran fluttering
like a little girl
after her mother

> Sappho (b. 612 B.C.?), in *Sappho: A New Transla-*
> *tion,* trans. Mary Barnard, 1958

Centuries of custom, centuries of precedent! They pressed, they crushed, they suffocated ... They *must* swim against the current; it was ridiculous, preposterous that because she did not marry she should be forced to live a crippled existence. What real difference could it possibly make to her mother's loneliness if her daughter shared a flat with Elizabeth instead of with a husband? No difference at all, except in precedent.

> Radclyffe Hall, on Joan's desire for a life with
> Elizabeth rather than with the man who proposed
> to her. *The Unlit Lamp,* 1924

Tessa continued, "Sydney is very affectionate."

"She is very much ... absorbed, isn't she, by Mrs. Kerr?"

"I have known *other* cases," said somebody else, looking about vaguely for her scissors, "of these very violent friendships. One didn't feel *those others* were quite healthy."

"I should discourage any daughter of mine from a friendship with an older woman. It is never the best women who have these strong influences. I would far rather she lost her head about a man."

> Elizabeth Bowen, *The Hotel,* 1928

My mother was told that I was living a lesbian life with Valerie. All she had to say was that I was living a lesbian life and that was grounds to have you committed to an insane asylum ... I was picked up off the streets, thrown in a police car, and [they] put me down into the psycho ward of the general hospital.

> Donna Smith, of the homophobia she experienced in the 1930s, quoted in Andrea Weiss and Greta Schiller, *Before Stonewall*, 1988

In loving another woman I discovered the deep urge to both be a mother and find a mother in my lover. At first I feared the discovery. Everything around me told me it was evil ... Now, I treasure and trust the drama between two loving women...

> Sue Silvermarie, "The Motherhood," in *Women: A Journal of Liberation* 4(1), 1974

The overthrow of what the mother has become in our culture through centuries of oppression is basic to the emergence of a new as yet embryonic reality of self. The mother has become ... domineering, overprotective, unfulfilled, frustrated, projective, living her life through others...

> Jill Johnston, on the lesbian's struggle to "convert or neutralize" the mother within and the real parental mother, in *Ms.*, June 1975

There is no intimacy between woman and woman which is not preceded by a long narrative of the mother.

> Bertha Harris, *Lover*, 1976

The daughters never were
true brides of the father

the daughters were to begin with
brides of the mother

then brides of each other
under a different law

> Adrienne Rich, "Sibling Mysteries," 1976, *The Dream of a Common Language*, 1978

I flung at you the dirtiest word from any gutter
LESBIAN
you cannot understand how
it happened
your angelic stringbean girl of satin ribbons
making skirts for toni dolls

> Ellen Marie Bissert, "mother," *The Immaculate Conception of the Blessed Virgin Dyke,* 1977

I am one of those wimmin for whom there was never any doubt about my sexuality: I've always loved wimmin, and my mother was my first womonlove. My first conscious expression of my Lesbianism occurred when I was four or five.

> Julia Penelope Stanley, in Julia Penelope Stanley and Susan J. Wolfe, eds., *The Coming Out Stories,* 1980

Mother and daughter embrace through the bars of patriarchal authority that imprisons them both. The rule of the man's world always mediates between them: from mother to daughter, from daughter to her own daughter. Lesbianism can be seen as rejection of the traditional, nuclear family paradigm that has fostered this relationship.

> Jill Dolan, 1983, quoted in Rosemary Curb, in Karla Jay and Joanne Glasgow, eds., *Lesbian Texts and Contexts,* 1990

Lesbian ... No word more terrifying, in my mother's mouth it is a snake hissing, Lesbian, intake of breath the unspeakable word.

> Kate Millett, *Flying,* 1990

...Maybe you'll marry a doctor. Keep up your maths. Learn to follow the share market. Always finish what you start. If a job's worth doing, it's worth doing well. Have you fed the dogs, watered the garden, swept the back path, cleaned the aviary? Virgins shouldn't use tampons.

Why did you turn out to be a lesbian?

> Susan Hawthorne, "Mother/Girl," in Cathie Duns-ford and Susan Hawthorne, eds., *The Exploding Frangipani,* 1990

FAMILY

When we were growing up, most of our parents, when they found out we were gay, we were excommunicated from the family, or we were just totally dropped. We weren't invited to a lot of family affairs. My mother tore up my brother's wedding invitation to me because she didn't want the "queer" coming to the wedding.

> Marge Summit, on growing up lesbian and gay in the 1950s, quoted in Andrea Weiss and Greta Schiller, *Before Stonewall,* 1988

i want to tell them: my back is healing,
i dream of dragons and water.
my home is in her arms,
our bedroom ceiling the wide open sky.

> Kitty Tsui, "A Chinese Banquet," in Carl Morse and Joan Larkin, eds., *Gay and Lesbian Poetry in our Time,* 1988

I still find it difficult to believe that I was produced by my parents. I feel as if I invented myself ... I don't know if perhaps being lesbian makes you see the world differently. That you never see yourself as this one static being...

> Elsa Beckett, in an oral history in Hall Carpenter Archives Lesbian Oral History Group, *Inventing Ourselves,* 1989

Many parents of both sexes see "contagious" lesbianism as a greater threat to their daughters than the danger of rape, alcoholism, drugs, or Communism.

> Mary Meigs, in Karla Jay and Joanne Glasgow, eds., *Lesbian Texts and Contexts,* 1990

My parents have no problem with my being a lesbian, because my parents are lesbians.

> Jennifer DiMarco, quoted in *The Advocate,* January 12, 1993

HUSBANDS

...had Ann lived, it is probable she would never have loved Henry so fondly; but if she had, she could not have talked of her passion to any human creature. She deliberated, and at last informed the family, that she had a reason for not living with her husband, which must for some time remain a secret – they stared – Not live with him!

> Mary Wollstonecraft, describing Mary's commitment to Ann, *Mary, a Fiction,* 1788

With only a minimal qualm, she renounced Kay's friendship and whatever possibilities it might hold of emotional involvement. "I'll leave the receiver off the hook," she decided firmly. Bill smiled down at her. "Want to go somewhere and sit down?"

She slipped her hand into his. "All I want," she said softly, "is to go home – with you."

> Valerie Taylor, Frankie and Bill, *Stranger on Lesbos*, 1960. Frankie is abandoning her lover, Kay, to return to her husband, Bill, who earlier had raped her in a fit of rage.

"I don't know what David will do, Maggie. He could still destroy us."

"I'll take my chances," Maggie replied. "I can face anything as long as you're with me."

"I love you," Jenny said. "I'll be with you as long as you want me."

> Evelyn Kennedy, *Of Love and Glory*, 1989. Jenny is leaving her husband, David, for Maggie.

GAY MEN

...there is little intermingling between the male and female homosexual societies. At the parties, at the bars, among one's friends and friends' friends, it is rare to meet Lesbians.

> Donald W. Cory, *The Homosexual in America*, 1951

The front marriage is not quite as universally appealing as it would seem, and even if, as some people believe, Lesbianism were as common as male homosexuality, and even if males and females in this submerged world freely intermingled, such marriages, in my opinion would not be frequent occurrences. For the Lesbian cannot offer hope for an avenue of escape that so many homosexuals are seeking...

> Donald W. Cory, *The Homosexual in America*, 1951

The "gay girl" is neither in temperament or in action much like the gay fellow. In general she is rarely to be seen in bars or other night spots, nor is she frequently even in large groups ... She is a stay at home, or if of the barring type, inhabiting small mixed bars.

> M.F., "Discussion, Anyone?," in the *Homosexual Magazine One,* February 1954

...the act male homosexuals commit is ugly and repugnant and afterwards they are disgusted with themselves. They drink and take drugs, to palliate this, but they are disgusted with the act and they are always changing partners and cannot be really happy. In women it is the opposite. They do nothing that they are disgusted by and nothing that is repulsive and afterwards they are happy and they can lead happy lives together.

> Gertrude Stein, quoted in Ernest Hemingway, *A Moveable Feast,* 1964

Lesbians are women first and homosexuals second. They have far more in common with their heterosexual sisters than with their male counterparts.

> Denise M. Cronin, in Erich Goode and Richard R. Troiden, eds., *Sexual Deviance and Sexual Deviants,* 1974

Male homosexual literature has a past, it has a present. The lesbians, for their part, are silent – just as all women are as women at all levels. When one has read the poems of Sappho, Radclyffe Hall's *Well of Loneliness,* the poems of Sylvia Plath and Anaïs Nin, *La Bâtarde* by Violette Leduc, one has read everything.

> Monique Wittig, *The Lesbian Body,* 1975

The only thing that lesbians and male homosexuals have in common is the civil rights issue. I don't see what males see in each other.

> Jill Johnston, in *Ms.*, June 1975

By splitting along genital differences, lesbians and gay men have totally inherited the legacies of sexist childhood. We emulate straight society, where men and women rarely speak their truths.

> Loretta Lotman, in *Gotham,* July 8, 1976

In contrast to the time, money, and attention paid to male homosexuality, relatively little is known about female homosexuality...

> Donna Tanner, *The Lesbian Couple,* 1978

Lesbians are typically feminine in much of their behavior, for example they court each other for long periods of time, sex is approved of only when it occurs within an emotional relationship, the community is organized around couples. This is in complete contrast to gay men's often noted promiscuity and single status.

> Martin P. Levine, ed., *Gay Men,* 1979

Entertaining Mr. Sloane, The Madness of Lady Bright and *T-Shirts* promulgate the typical gay man's promiscuity; *Confessions of a Female Disorder* and *A Late Snow* display the hyper-romanticism/submerged sexuality that seems endemic to lesbians.

> Don Shewey, in *Christopher Street,* May 1979

Lesbians have historically been deprived of a political existence through "inclusion" as female versions of male homosexuality. To equate lesbian existence with male homosexuality because each is stigmatized is to erase female reality once again.

> Adrienne Rich, "Compulsory Heterosexuality and Lesbian Existence," 1980, *Blood, Bread, and Poetry,* 1986

... When lesbians assert themselves they are asserting themselves as women; when gay men assert themselves, it is, at least in part, in opposition to the expected superiority of men. Thus gay men are visible as gay in a way that is less true for lesbians...

> Dennis Altman, *The Homosexualization of America, The Americanization of the Homosexual,* 1982

At this particular moment in history when the ratios of sexual preference seem to have gone awry and vast numbers of homosexual men and straight single women are roaming the range in search of love, sex and meaningful relations, it is obvious that these two groups dress up to enhance their sexual attraction while lesbian women and heterosexual men dress more carelessly or to conceal their bodies, having no urgent need to attract the judgmental male eye.

> Susan Brownmiller, *Femininity,* 1984

It's a little different for women than for men. I think men who are gay are a little more committed to being gay ... For women, especially when you're in your 30s, you start having these maternal feelings...

> Sandra Bernhard, on why she thinks lesbians are more bisexual than gay men, quoted in *Outlines,* August 1990

If I were asked to describe the difference between the sexes in the gay world, I would say that the men wanted to be amused; the girls sought vindication.

> Quentin Crisp, quoted in William Cole and Louis Phillips, eds., *Sex: "The Most Fun You Can Have without Laughing" and Other Quotations,* 1990

Gay male sex ... is *articulate* ... Lesbian "sex" as I have known it, most of the time I have known it, is utterly *in*articulate ... I have, in effect, no linguistic community, no language ... no knowledge.

> Marilyn Frye, on lesbians' lack of a sexual vocabulary, in Jeffner Allen, ed., *Lesbian Philosophies and Cultures,* 1990

A lesbian in the gay community is exposed to more gay male sex fantasies than most heterosexual women are to straight men's. I speculate that gay men have become fetishized sex symbols in many sexual fantasies.

> Julia Creet, in *Out/Look,* Winter 1991

One of the great frustrations lesbians have with gay men is our lack of knowledge and interest about their lives.

> John Preston, *The Big Gay Book,* 1991

Lesbians organize as lesbians, just as gay men organize as gay men. But lesbians also organize as oppressed women. Their politics and their culture reflect this double vision.

> Sy Adler and Johanna Brenner, in the *International Journal of Urban and Regional Research,* March 1992

I'm basically a homosexual man. I love clothes. I love good, fine fabrics. I work out. I'm concerned about my looks. I'm vain.

> Sarah Jessica Parker, quoted in *The Advocate,* January 12, 1993

With all my heart, I don't want to die of AIDS, and it's gonna happen because of these 12 years of criminal neglect. I'm glad I've lived long enough to experience the joyous coming together of gay men and lesbians...

> Paul Monette, quoted in *Out,* April/May 1993

There was so much interaction between gay men and lesbians that a network of caring and compassion arose. I have seen lesbians who never gave a darn about men or gay men, holding gay men who are dying.

> Torie Osborn, on how the AIDS epidemic has brought gay men and lesbians together, quoted in *New York,* May 10, 1993

COMING OUT

I'm very glad to be here. It's been kind of a long trip ... I've wanted to be here, I suppose, in a surreptitious way for a long time, and I was always too chicken ... Anyway, I'm out of the closet. Here I am.

> Kate Millett, in a speech to the Daughters of Bilitis, quoted in Merle Miller, *On Being Different,* 1971

...at some point I believe one has to stop holding back for fear of alienating some imaginary reader or real relative or friend, and come out with personal truth.

> May Sarton, *Journal of a Solitude,* 1973

Nowadays it's very fashionable to come out of the closet. I read where an athlete recently came out and said he was gay. So what? I know 50,000 athletes who are queer as a bat. How is that kind of publicity going to affect his family, his friends? I'm not sure it's a responsible thing to do.

> Johnny Mathis, 1976, quoted in *The Advocate*, October 6, 1992

I think coming out is a life-long process.

> Caryl B. Bentley, in Julia Penelope Stanley and Susan J. Wolfe, eds., *The Coming Out Stories,* 1980

I don't tell people that they have to come out, but the least they can do is work for the community. They can lick stamps or send letters.

> Robin Tyler, quoted in Val Edwards, in Ed Jackson and Stan Persky, eds., *Flaunting It!,* 1982

I am absolutely convinced that if everyone would come out at once and stay out we could put an end to most of our problems.

> Barbara Grier, in Margaret Cruikshank, ed., *The Lesbian Path,* 1985

Lesbian nuns I know are going to dance! In convents this book will go around like hotcakes, just the way *The Hite Report* did.

> Sister Sara, predicting how the book *Lesbian Nuns,* in which nuns come out, would be received, quoted in Rosemary Curb and Nancy Manahan, eds., *Lesbian Nuns,* 1985

Come out for yourself
Come out for your friends
Come out for justice

> Message on a poster advertising the National March on Washington for Gay and Lesbian Rights, October 11, 1987

When I came out
to her   she started
calling me
you people

> Jane Barnes, "Homophobia," in Christian McEwen,
> ed., *Naming the Waves*, 1988

Three years ago while stirring spaghetti sauce, I said to myself, "I'm a lesbian."

> René Cliff, in Harriet Alpert, ed., *We Are Every-where*, 1988

Out of the Closets and Into the Universe

> Slogan of the Gaylaxian Science Fiction Society,
> quoted in *Outlines*, December 1989

I regard the greatest villains today to be those famous closet cases who are not being open about their lives. These people could make an enormous difference in enlightening the general public about the nature of homosexuality. And I'm tired of hearing their feeble excuses for why this isn't possible. It almost always boils down to money in the long run.

> Armistead Maupin, to Australia's *Outrage*, quoted
> in *Outlines*, August 1990

I didn't come out until I was 30. My oldest brother had the most trouble with my being a lesbian ... When I first came out to him he told me, "Don't tell Dad. It will kill him." This gave me visions of myself as the neutron lesbian. "Hey, Mr. Reagan," I used to say onstage, "I'm a lesbian." *Kaboom!*

> Kate Clinton, 1990, quoted in *The Advocate*, Oc-
> tober 6, 1992

The entire future of a lesbian, or any gay person, lies in the few seconds of coming out, and the freedom one gains comes with a new experience of unforeseen penalties.

> Mary Meigs, in Karla Jay and Joanne Glasgow, eds.,
> *Lesbian Texts and Contexts,* 1990

The writer-lesbian, or indeed any lesbian who has come out of the closet, must learn to live with the role of scapegoat; she must develop special gills for breathing homophobic air, special muscles for a robust sense of humor.

> Mary Meigs, in Karla Jay and Joanne Glasgow, eds.,
> *Lesbian Texts and Contexts,* 1990

I have a pile of books on my table: gay and lesbian history, older lesbians speaking, Vito Russo, Judy Grahn, Cherríe Moraga, and a lot more. A straight friend of mine came in here and said, "Oh, are you studying to be a lesbian?" It's funny but true. I haven't been around that long as a lesbian.

> Yvonne Rainer, on how life changed after coming out at age 56, in an interview in *The Advocate,* November 5, 1991

In coming out, a person acts to create a sense of wholeness by establishing congruence between interior experience and external presentation, moving the inner into the outer, bringing the hidden to light, and transforming a private into a social reality. The closet symbolizes isolation, the individual without society, a stranger even to self.

> Kath Weston, *Families We Choose,* 1991

There's something I've been wanting to tell you for a while. I am a L-L-L L-awrence Welk fan.

> k.d. lang, during a concert at Radio City Music Hall, August 26, 1992, quoted in the *New York Times,* August 28, 1992

There are well-known people who have come out quietly and bravely and gone on with their lives. Women like Martina Navratilova, k.d. lang, and Linda Villarosa (an editor of *Essence*). These women chose to stop evading or lying about their lives...

> Victoria A. Brownworth, in *The Advocate,* April 20, 1993

It was a gradual process that took several months. But I can remember writing in my journal: I'm a lesbian and I can no longer deny it.

> Torie Osborn, on coming out of the closet in 1972, quoted in the *New York Times,* April 24, 1993

I say to you still trapped in the prisons called closets: we are waiting for you and come out you must. Your secrecy is killing you. It's killing us. And it's killing the dream called America.

> Torie Osborn, in a speech at the March on Washington for Lesbian, Gay, and Bi Equal Rights, April 25, 1993

...to all lesbian and gay actors in Hollywood and on Broadway, do yourselves a favor, join us, come out of the closet now.

> Sir Ian McKellen, in a speech at the March on Washington for Lesbian, Gay, and Bi Equal Rights, April 25, 1993

What our movement for equality needs most, in my not so humble opinion, is for us to come out of the closet ... Let's come out and dispel the rumors and lies that are being spread about us. Let's come out and set everybody straight, so to speak.

> Martina Navratilova, in a speech at the March on Washington for Lesbian, Gay, and Bi Equal Rights, April 25, 1993

...I just told everyone. I literally was going into people's offices and saying, "Good morning, I'm a lesbian..."

> Linda Villarosa, quoted in *New York,* May 10, 1993

T he more people come out, the less it will be an issue. If we are ashamed of ourselves, how the hell can we expect the rest of the world not to be ashamed of us?

> Martina Navratilova, quoted in *New York,* May 10, 1993

S exuality, whether homo or hetero, does not arrive only once, in that moment of revelation and proclamation that we call "coming out." Our body is always coming out. Every time is the first time. Every performance is a debut.

> Wayne Koestenbaum, *The Queen's Throat,* 1993

OUTING

I t's a big mistake to live in disagreement with your sexuality. A horrid mistake. But the way of helping that person is not to call the press and say, "I know this person is gay." What you're doing in that case is traumatizing someone who hasn't solved a problem. To me, it seems like some kind of revenge. Someone who is closeted doesn't need press attention. I say, help them get psychiatric treatment to come to terms with it.

> Pedro Almovadar, to *The Advocate,* quoted in *Outlines,* August 1990

O *utWeek* is not a magazine ... This is pure, undiluted invasion. It's damaging, it's immoral, it's McCarthyism, it's terrorism, it's cannibalism, it's beneath contempt.

> Fran Lebowitz, on her dislike for *OutWeek* and its promotion of outing, to *The Advocate,* quoted in *Outlines,* August 1990

If you want to trash something, trash the homophobes because that's where the problem is. Gay performers aren't doing anything wrong.

> Gretchen Phillips of the group Two Nice Girls, on whether musicians should be outed, quoted in *Ms.,* November/December 1991

LESBIAN SANCTUARIES

Of course we could walk out of the bar
but then we wouldnt be lesbians
Out there was the world of lies
Here we could be ourselves
I came here to meet my sisters
my world

> Fran Winant, "Happy New Year," *Looking at Women,* 1971

Most Lesbians are intensely aware of the limitations of their gay resources. Sanctuaries – inadequate, temporary, often sordid – act as reminders of their dilemma and dramatize the need to make it in the larger world, or to create a larger world.

> Sidney Abbott and Barbara Love, *Sappho Was a Right-on Woman,* 1972

The bars came closest to being a community and a social institution, but not very close. They were violent, confusing, expensive, and exploiting. They gave lesbianism a bad name. They manufactured the worst lesbian stereotypes...

> Eleanor Cooper, in Ginny Vida, ed., *Our Right to Love,* 1978

The bars are more than imperfect, more than unfortunate. They represent lives spent in complicit and habitual superficiality. Superficiality is a breed of silence, and silence has a long history in us: most of us have spent the larger portion of our lives denying the fact of our existence.

> Felice Newman, in Karla Jay and Allen Young, eds., *Lavender Culture,* 1978

GROWING UP LESBIAN

We need our own "Save the Children Campaign." I want to save *our* children, all the little kids out there who are going to grow up to be homosexual and lesbian ... Society talks about not aborting fetuses ... but in the name of religion they abort people constantly, they abort hopes and desires.

> Robin Tyler, quoted in the *Lesbian Tide,* September/October 1978

Yes, I was a teen-age lesbian.

> Jeanne Cordova, in Margaret Cruikshank, ed., *The Lesbian Path,* 1985

65% of gay runaways ... encountered physical or sexual abuse in their homes, 80% said they are involved in prostitution, 95% said they have problems with drugs, alcohol, or both, and almost 60% said they have attempted suicide.

> R.W. Peterson, in *The Advocate,* April 11, 1989

Where were the stories of tomboys? Of little kids growing up with same sex or single parents? Why did Nancy Drew have to have a boyfriend? Why couldn't a writer portray puppy love between best girlfriends? ... Did Jill never save Jack? Or Jane, Jill?

> Lee Lynch, in Karla Jay and Joanne Glasgow, eds., *Lesbian Texts and Contexts,* 1990

According to a 1989 U.S. Health and Human Services Report on youth suicide, gays account for 30 percent of the 5,000 suicides committed in America every year by people aged 15 to 24. That's a lot of dead kids, citizens who are obliterated in a war far deadlier and more insidious than any trumped-up invasion of foreign soils.

> Lee Lynch, in *Just Out* (Portland, Oregon), quoted in *TWN,* May 13, 1992

For many lesbian and gay teenagers growing up in rural America, the prospect of coming out in their communities is almost unthinkable. While there is a wealth of resources for gay youth in cities like New York, San Francisco, and Los Angeles, the majority of smaller towns across the country offer little more than stereotypes and invisibility to young lesbians and gays.

> Shira Maguen, in *The Advocate,* November 17, 1992

The National Network of Runaway and Youth Services (NNRYS), a private advocacy group, estimates that anywhere from a quarter to a half million lesbian, gay, and bisexual youth in this country run away or are pushed out of their homes annually.

> Liz Galst, in *The Advocate,* December 29, 1992

I resent like hell that I was maybe eighteen before I ever heard the "L" word. It would have made all the difference for me had I grown up knowing that the reason I didn't fit in was because they hadn't told me there were more categories to fit into.

> Michelle Shocked, April 1990, quoted in Leigh W. Rutledge, *The Gay Decades,* 1992

As a teenager I didn't see any positive gay images. I wasn't able to find them. And they certainly weren't in my high school curriculum. But I remember getting excited by characters in books who were marginally alluded to as gay. I also went to Rock

Hudson and Doris Day movies and spent my time focusing on Doris, putting myself in Rock's place. I was thinking about kissing Doris, rather than kissing Rock.

> Ann Northrop, in Eric Marcus, ed., *Making History,* 1992

When I was 21, I was terrified. These young lesbians aren't scared in the same way. They're living their lives instead of explaining their lives.

> Dorothy Allison, quoted in *Newsweek,* June 21, 1993

FROM CONVENTS TO COLLEGES

...When I first left home to attend a boarding school, I was willing in my loneliness to have a "little friendship." So I fell in love just like a boy, and wooed and won, as a friend and a good one, a sweet tempered, sweetfaced girl.

> Mary Willard, on a love affair at North Western Female College in the late 1850s and early 1860s, quoted in Nancy Sahli, *Chrysalis,* Summer 1979

When a Vassar girl takes a shine to another, she straightway enters upon a regular course of bouquet sendings, interspersed with tinted notes, mysterious packages of "Ridley's Mixed Candies," locks of hair perhaps, and many other tender tokens, until at last the object of her attentions is captured, the two become inseparable, and the aggressor is considered by her circle of acquaintances as – *smashed.*

> A Yalie's description of relationships between young women at Vassar in the *Yale Courant,* the Yale student newspaper, 1873. Quoted in Nancy Sahli, *Chrysalis,* Summer 1979

If the "smash" is mutual, they monopolize each other & "spoon" continually, & sleep together & lie awake all night talking instead of going to sleep; & if it isn't mutual the unrequited one cries herself sick ... My theory is that it comes of massing hundreds of nervous young girls together, & shutting them up from the outside world.

> Alice Stone Blackwell, in a letter to the Association of Collegiate Alumnae Committee about "smashes" in women's colleges, 1882. Quoted in Nancy Sahli, in *Chrysalis,* Summer 1979

I was becoming more and more worried because I was not like other girls, so I felt that I had better get married as soon as my school days were over, and become normal, as it was supposed that a girl who had sweethearts and wanted to be married was wholly normal. My interest in girls persisted, however, and I could not get up much enthusiasm over the marriage idea.

> Mary Casal, on her attraction to young women in college in the late nineteenth century, *The Stone Wall,* 1930

These bunches of women living together, falling in love with each other because they haven't anyone else to fall in love with! It's obscene! Oh, take me away!

> Marion Patton, Lydia to her fiancé upon departing a women's college, *Dance on the Tortoise,* 1930

This is the town of South Hadley,
The place where the faculty pray,
Where Chuckie speaks only to Jeannette
And Jeannette speaks only to May.

> Verse popular at Mount Holyoke College in 1932, quoted in Anna Mary Wells, *Miss Marks and Miss Woolley,* 1978

I feel very much at home in the Catholic colleges. The most radical women today are nuns. They really are.

> May Sarton, in an interview with Margaret Cruikshank, in *The Advocate,* August 18, 1983

W e convent schoolgirls were heroic lovers, unsupported explorers.
What we did put us outside the world we knew
and for a time we held together.

> Caroline Griffin, "Elizabeth," in Barbara Burford, Lindsay MacRae, and Sylvia Paskin, eds., *Dancing the Tightrope,* 1987

I think that at some time in every girl's life, there's another girl in school whom you cannot cease admiring. She's bright, she's funny, her socks are just right, and if she chooses to walk down the hall with you, you float. And that's a crush, and girls have crushes on other girls in school. Usually women outgrow that. Sometimes they don't.

> Victoria Principal, in an interview in *People,* quoted in *TWN,* February 22, 1989

...there is every reason to believe that "coming out" on campus as lesbian or gay – and thus obtaining the crucial support of others – will be met with physical and psychological harassment.

> Anthony R. D'Augelli, in the *Journal of Interpersonal Violence,* September 1992

THE LESBIAN LOOK

Miss Butler is tall and masculine, she wears always a riding habit, hangs her hat with the air of a sportsman in the hall, and appears in all respects as a young man if we except the petticoats which she still retains. Miss Ponsonby, on the contrary, is polite so effeminate, fair and beautiful.

> Of Eleanor Butler and Sarah Ponsonby (also known as the Ladies of Llangollen), in the *General Evening Post,* July 24, 1790. Quoted in Elizabeth Mavor, ed., *A Year with the Ladies of Llangollen,* 1986

Eighteen hundred and thirty one ... exactly a century has passed since the death of [Sarah Ponsonby]. Can we possibly, without apprehension, imagine two ladies of Llangollen in this year of 1930? They would own a car, wear dungarees, smoke cigarettes, have short hair, and there would be a liquor bar in their apartment. Would Sarah Ponsonby still know how to remain silent? Perhaps, with the aid of crossword puzzles. Eleanor Butler would curse as she jacked up the car, and would have her breasts amputated.

> Sidonie Gabrielle Colette, *Ces plaisirs,* 1932

Miss Radclyffe Hall was a strange but impressive-looking woman, short of stature, with a disproportionately large but handsomely shaped head and always with a perfect haircut. Her hands and feet were also large, as were the beautiful sapphires which she wore, one as a finger ring and one each as a cuff link. She wore beautifully tailored English suits, tight-fitting across the bosom and shoulders...

> Janet Flanner, on Radclyffe Hall's attire, in *Paris Was Yesterday 1925–1939,* ed. I. Drutman, 1972

The lesbian gaze is a transgressive act.

> Michel Foucault, in *Language, Counter-Memory, Practice,* ed. Donald F. Bouchard, 1977

Ironically groups of nuns or Lesbians are often mistaken for one another today, since we often travel in female packs oblivious to male attention or needs.

> Rosemary Curb, in Rosemary Curb and Nancy Manahan, eds., *Lesbian Nuns,* 1985

"It's those two new girls on the block, Harold, something about the way they walk, something about the way they talk ... something about the way they look ... at each other ... Harold, I could swear they're Lebanese!"

> Holly Hughes, Louise to Harold, *The Well of Horniness,* in Don Shewey, ed., *Out Front,* 1988

Every man should own at least one dress – and so should lesbians.

> Jane Adams Spahr, 1988, quoted in Leigh W. Rutledge, *The Gay Decades,* 1992

The Gay method is to wear earrings out of balance. For Lesbians, this could be one in one ear only; two in one ear and three in the other or some other unequal match.

> "Things My Mother Never Told Me," in *Scene Out* (Manchester), August 1989

There is no longer a clear one-to-one correspondence between fashion and identity. For many, clothes are transient, interchangeable; you can dress as a femme one day and a butch the next. You can wear a crew-cut along with a skirt.

> Arlene Stein, in *Out/Look,* Winter 1989

...lesbian bodies are reputed to be stout, broad-shouldered, thunder-thighed, and athletic. Their body movements are graceless and abrupt. Their handshake – as well as their vaginal grip, according to William Burroughs – could crush a lead pipe.

Marshall Kirk and Hunter Madsen, on society's distorted picture of lesbians, *After the Ball,* 1989

...lesbians don't have horns or flashing neon signs.

Lorraine Trenchard, *Being Lesbian,* 1989

Today's lesbian "self" is a thoroughly urban creature who interprets fashion as something to be worn and discarded. Nothing is sacred for very long. Constantly changing, she dabbles in fashion, constructing one self after another, expressing her desires in a continual process of experimentation.

Inge Blackman and Kathryn Perry, in the *Feminist Review,* Spring 1990

Dress and Plumage. "Ms. Macha," or "The Plaid-Bellied Lumber-Jill Species": denims (baggy); overalls (especially with brass snaps); work shirts (muted tones); bill-fronted caps; backpacks (never, ever a purse!); leather jackets with zip pockets, combat boots, hiking boots, tie-oxfords (scuffy), or, on a rare occasion, saddle shoes, or sneakers...

Patricia Roth Schwartz, in Ann E. Larson and Carole A. Carr, eds., *Silverleaf's Choice: An Anthology of Lesbian Humor,* 1990

On 12th Street in Brooklyn, a Catholic schoolgirl in a brown plaid uniform smoking a Camel passed me and exhaled, "Faggot."

Jeanette Coon, in *OutWeek,* July 3, 1991

Women-sensible shoes, lilac or pink colours, Eau Dynami-sante, turned-up collar, odd earrings, no handbag, no lipstick or bright lipstick, short hair or very long, trousers or an ethnic skirt, no fat wedding ring, Dutch, has shoulders back, a tattoo, makes eye contact, chats about tennis, motorbikes or football.

"Gay Spotting Guide to the Universe," in *Pink Times* (Oxford), Autumn 1991

...the most telling clue when looking for Lesbians is eye contact ... If the woman looks back, holding contact instead of letting her gaze slide quickly away, she is probably a Lesbian.

Marilyn Murphy, *Are You Girls Traveling Alone?*, 1991

So what does a Lesbian look like? Well, we saw two old women drive into a campground in a large motor home. One dog and no men accompanied them. These are Lesbian-positive clues.

Marilyn Murphy, *Are You Girls Traveling Alone?*, 1991

In the early '80s we dressed a certain way to identify ourselves to each other. Now, in the '90s, we're dressing to show the world who we are.

Urvashi Vaid, quoted in *The Advocate,* January 28, 1992

There's the butch/femme camp, the kids who are enamored of the sixties look, the punk-and-leather crowd, the hip downtown black leather crowd, the very p.c., seventies-style feminists, and the glamour lesbians.

Diane Salvatore, quoted in *New York,* May 10, 1993

PARENTING

"Childless" women have been burned as witches, persecuted as lesbians, have been refused the right to adopt children because they were unmarried. They have been seen as embodiments of the great threat to male hegemony: the woman who is not tied to the family, who is disloyal to the law of heterosexual pairing and bearing.

Adrienne Rich, *Of Woman Born,* 1976

To lie to our children degrades both us and them. The openly lesbian mother is not only breaking a taboo; she is rebelling against the tradition that says that parents should lie to their children, that children do not merit the truth.

Adrienne Rich, in the Foreword to Bernice Good-man, *The Lesbian,* 1977

The future is the lesbian mother as a statement of the exciting diversity necessary for life on our planet. The future is the children that the lesbian mother will raise in the dignity of difference.

Bernice Goodman, *The Lesbian,* 1977

It is interesting that lesbians who choose not to be mothers are rarely, if ever, subjected to the kind of social pressure their heterosexual counterparts experience when making the same decision. So often, it is simply assumed that lesbians don't like kids...

Cheri Pies, *Considering Parenthood,* 1985

To mother as a lesbian is to choose to be different. To mother a son as a lesbian is to be different from the world and my child — while trying to balance it all.

Maria Starr, in Harriet Alpert, ed., *We Are Everywhere,* 1988

I believe that lesbians should not be bearing and raising boy children ... Lesbians should not put valuable energy into raising the oppressor ... The heteropatriarchal cult of motherhood also brings privilege. When you are seen with your child your lesbianism is invisible to the heteropatriarchy. This privilege is at the expense of other lesbians.

> Elizabeth Braeman, in *Off Our Backs,* quoted in *Outlines,* December 1989

Heather's favorite number is two. She has two arms, two legs, two eyes, two ears, two hands and two feet. Heather has two pets: a ginger colored cat named Gingersnap and a big black dog named Midnight. Heather also has two mommies: Mama Jane and Mama Kate.

> Lesléa Newman, *Heather Has Two Mommies,* 1989

...a child told nothing about her mother's homosexuality can only relate to a fantasized parental image based on deceit and misinformation, even though her mother's intentions may have been the best in the world.

> Rip Corley, *The Final Closet,* 1990

I remember being struck by the fact that the negative reviews of *Of Woman Born,* my prose book about motherhood, tended to use the fact that I wrote as a lesbian to undercut everything I had to say about being a mother. You know, sort of this idea that lesbians are not mothers, or if lesbians are mothers, they're unfit mothers, and so no wonder that this lesbian is trying to undermine the mythology, the ideology of motherhood as we would have it.

> Adrienne Rich, in an interview in *The Advocate,* December 31, 1991

Even in the wake of national publicity about custody cases and the lesbian baby boom, many heterosexuals still do not recognize the potential for lesbians and gay men to become involved in child care and co-parenting arrangements, much less view them as persons capable of producing biological offspring.

Kath Weston, *Families We Choose,* 1991

When it's time to go home, Mama Rose and Mama Grace hold hands as we walk to the rainbow of balloons. I look at my mommies and I feel happy because we had so much fun. I wish we didn't have to wait another whole year for Gay Pride Day to come again.

Lesléa Newman, *Gloria Goes to Gay Pride,* 1991

There are an estimated eight to ten million children being raised in three million gay- and lesbian-headed households in the United States.

Virginia Casper, Steven Schultz, and Elaine Wickens, in *Teachers College Record,* Fall 1992

Love Makes a Family

Message on a pin spotted at the Lambda Rising bookstore in Washington, D.C., 1993

GROWING OLDER

Again I was outside, again I was "other." Again I lived with the never-knowing when people would turn away from me, not because they had identified me as a lesbian, since I was no longer thought of as a sexual being, but because they had identified me as old. I had lived my life without novels, movies, radio, or television telling me that lesbians existed or that it was possible to be glad to be a lesbian. Now nothing told me that old women existed, or that it was possible to be glad to be an old woman. Again the silence held powerful and repressive messages.

> Barbara MacDonald with Cynthia Rich, *Look Me in the Eye,* 1984

I may have to go on calling myself a lesbian into great old age, not because it is any longer true but because it takes such a long time to make the simple point that I have the right to be.

> Jane Rule, *A Hot-Eyed Moderate,* 1985

Ageing means freedom from playing the "fool the males game" – freedom from borrowed engagement rings, from contrived male lovers, from the intense social pressures to act out the traditional female role.

> Anonymous, "Admissions of Mortality: The Pleasures and Problems of Lesbian Athletes," in Marcy Adelman, ed., *Long Time Passing,* 1986

Unless old lesbians are re-membered as sexual, attractive, useful, integral parts of the woman-loving world, then current lesbian identity is a temporary mirage, not a new social statement of female empowerment.

> Baba Copper, *Ageism in the Lesbian Community,* 1987

It takes a lot of consciousness and effort for older lesbians to build and maintain support networks so [we don't become] lonely, bored, and depressed. We learn to build our relationships without the same kind of passionate intimacy that we had when younger.

> Ruth Morales, quoted in Marcy Adelman, "Quieting Our Fears: Lesbians and Aging," in *Out/Look,* Fall 1988

Older lesbians who are out are frequently not acknowledged, sought after, or listened to. Especially when ageism is compounded by racism or classism, the older lesbian may feel alienated from the very group she reaches out to.

> D. Merilee Clunis and G. Dorsey Green, *Lesbian Couples,* 1988

Ageing does affect every aspect of life. It can bring couples closer together or tear them apart. Gay and lesbian lovers are well advised to expand their social connections as far as possible to prevent gradual isolation as life continues.

> Tina Tessina, *Gay Relationships for Men and Women,* 1989

Conforming to the Little Old Lady stereotype of absolute powerlessness should not be a goal for any lesbian, yet the pressure I feel going "over the hill" is to behave less assertively – to be "appropriately" submissive ... Although old lesbians often receive deference, I seldom experience a feeling of real respect from others.

> Baba Copper, in Jeffner Allen, ed., *Lesbian Philosophies and Cultures,* 1990

Looking at the gap in her teeth, the mussed gray hair, and those brown eyes like mirrors full of desert roads and pickup trucks, honky-tonk gay bars and jukebox-dancing women, full of sixty-nine years of love and disappointment and love again, ah, jeeze, I knew I'd found somebody who was going to make all the mess and bother of love worthwhile – and I'm still grinning right back at her to this day.

> Lee Lynch, "Cactus Love," in Tina Portillo, ed., *Dykescapes,* 1991

The areas of concern for aging gay men and lesbians are primarily the same ones as for most aging adults – loneliness, health, and income ... However, the aging gay man and lesbian woman find another layer of concerns for the future ... rejection by adult children and grandchildren when as a parent or a grandparent they came out to their family.

> Jean K. Quam and Gary S. Whitford, in *Gerontologist*, June 1992

Lesbians are as guilty as the rest when it comes to the worship of youth. Even being thirty is considered a major obstacle, and we often don't think to include images of old lesbians in the things we produce.

> Suzanne Neild and Rosalind Pearson, *Women Like Us*, 1992

In the postmenopausal phase of life, many of us seem to be pulled toward reflection and integration, to introspection and to a more introverted kind of intimacy. We long for a relationship with another drawn in the same direction and have learned that such another is much more likely to be female than male.

> Christine Downing, in Robert H. Hopcke, Karin Lofthus Carrington, and Scott Wirth, eds., *Same-Sex Love and the Path to Wholeness*, 1993

HEALTH

Heterosexuality is a serious health hazard for women at this point in time.

> Frances Hornstein, *Lesbian Health Care*, 1973

Research confirms that being a Lesbian is beneficial to mental health.

> Cuca Hepburn with Bonnie Gutierrez, *Alive and Well: A Lesbian Health Guide*, 1988

ADDICTION

To some extent, all women are isolated from one another. Lesbians are often extremely isolated from each other and from the mainstream. To the extent that we are isolated, we are vulnerable to many other forms of violence including alcoholism.

> Nina Jo Smith, in Jean Swallow, ed., *Out from Under,* 1983

In the lesbian community, the bars are just a fantastic network of co-ing ... But the whole set-up pushes the drug called alcohol. So to take alcoholism out of its community base, we as a community have to build alternative structures to the bars to fulfill what the bar provides, which is socializing and networking.

> Celinda Cantu, in an interview in Jean Swallow, ed., *Out from Under,* 1983

As a lesbian I find that exercising constraint and experiencing subjugation are as much a part of my daily life as moving my body and breathing. I turned to addictions to help me keep my secret. And by adopting an addiction, by keeping my secret, I developed the ways to keep myself down – a pleasant demeanor, a martyr's stance, and a foggy brain.

> Susan Madden, in Margaret Cruikshank, ed., *The Lesbian Path,* 1985

Alcoholism stands out as a major health concern among lesbians. Statistically, between thirty and thirty-five percent of the lesbian community is troubled by alcohol abuse. This is about three times the national average for heterosexuals.

> Wayne R. Dynes, ed., *Encyclopedia of Homosexuality,* 1990

CANCER

The pain of separation from my breast was at least as sharp as the pain of separating from my mother. But I made it once before, so I know I can make it again.

Audre Lorde, in *Sinister Wisdom,* Spring 1979

Battling racism and battling heterosexism and battling apartheid share the same urgency inside me as battling cancer. None of these struggles are ever easy, and even the smallest victory is never to be taken for granted.

Audre Lorde, November 8, 1986, *A Burst of Light,* 1988

On Valentine's Day, February 14, 1988, Barbara Rosenblum died. She was my partner, my friend, my love. Now I sit at a computer trying to carve shape and substance into the cold marble of memory.

Sandra Butler, whose beloved companion died of cancer. When Barbara Rosenblum was diagnosed with breast cancer, the two began collaborating on this book, *Cancer in Two Voices,* 1991.

Cancer, like AIDS, is about living. It's about living with a life-threatening disease, in whatever state, in whatever condition...

Jackie Winnow, in the *Feminist Review,* Summer 1992

The 40,000 women [in the San Francisco Bay Area] with cancer don't have the services available to the 100 women with AIDS.

Jackie Winnow, in the *Feminist Review,* Summer 1992

As a community, we need to "come out" about cancer and its affect on lesbian women.

> Victoria A. Brownworth, in Midge Stocker, ed.,
> *Confronting Cancer, Confronting Change,* 1993

AIDS

I've now moved to a place where I can see trees and water. From here I'm recalling it all, my lover Joan's and my experience with AIDS. It's been a year since she was diagnosed, and she has been dead for eight months. I keep on hurting...

> Jennifer Brown, on her lover Joan Tedesco, who was diagnosed with AIDS in 1987 and shortly after committed suicide. In Ines Rieder and Patricia Ruppelt, eds., *AIDS: The Women,* 1988

The importance of making it clear that lesbianism is the safest sexuality around at present is not only to counter the homophobia generated by the fear of AIDS. It also highlights an inherent contradiction in the idea that AIDS is God's punishment for homosexuality.

> Diane Richardson, *Women and AIDS,* 1988

I'll do anything I can to draw attention to the cause, especially in a town like Washington which has chosen to ignore the disease, frankly. The government seems full of people who are enjoying the genocide of homosexuals. And please don't hesitate to quote me.

> Sandra Bernhard, at a June 1990 "Art against AIDS" gala in Washingon, D.C., quoted in *Outlines,* August 1990

Lesbians have been told they're a low risk group, yet defining risk in terms of groups rather than behavior is fatal. This has lulled us into a false sense of security and contributed to our denial that we are at risk for HIV ... This focus on the dental dam assumes that oral sex is the definitive characteristic of lesbian sex. Well, lesbian sex is much more than just eating pussy.

> Risa Denenberg, in *On Our Backs*, July/August 1991

Somebody in the lesbian community introduced the idea of dental dams, without any substantial discussion — scientific or social — about whether or not they were necessary. And because the community has historically behaved in a very faddish manner, people just went for it. And also because it really fit into a lot of people's shame about their sexuality. But the fact is, there isn't any evidence that HIV is transmitted through oral sex between women...

> Sara Schulman, in an interview in the *Bay Area Reporter*, quoted in *TWN*, May 13, 1992

Give me your living hand   If I could take the hour
death moved into you   undeclared, unnamed
—even if sweet, if I could take that hour
between my forceps   tear at it like a monster
wrench it out of your flesh   dissolve its shape in quicklime
and make you well again

> Adrienne Rich, "In Memoriam," in Michael Klein, ed., *Poets for Life*, 1992

He let it go too long. It's another aspect of his capacity for denial. He just didn't want to deal with it. He just didn't want to deal with homosexuality.

> Patti Davis, on Ronald Reagan's approach to AIDS, quoted in *The Advocate*, January 12, 1993

We would not be able to have the Year of the Queer, the decade of the '90s, if it were not for the last decade of the AIDS epidemic. That has created the incredible courage of people living with HIV. It has created such unstoppable, ferocious determination in all of us. It has telescoped what would have been decades of change.

> Torie Osborn, quoted in the *Village Voice,* April 27, 1993

BATTERING

The wall of silence surrounding lesbian battering has been virtually impenetrable, as has the wall of isolation, keeping lesbian victims separate from and unsupported by our community.

> Barbara Hart, in the Preface to Kerry Lobel, ed., *Naming the Violence,* 1986

Lesbians' silence about battering also reflects an acute awareness of societal homophobia. We fear feeling society's hatred and myths by speaking openly about lesbian battering. We fear hostile responses from police, courts, shelters, or therapists. Consequently, we are hesitant to call the police, seek counseling, or write articles.

> Mindy Benowitz, in Kerry Lobel, ed., *Naming the Violence,* 1986

Lesbians batter their lovers because violence is often an effective method to gain power and control over intimates.

> Barbara Hart, in Kerry Lobel, ed., *Naming the Violence,* 1986

Shame. Silence.
Not he.
She.
I didn't correct him.

> Chrystos, "'What Did He Hit You With?' The Doctor Said," in Kerry Lobel, ed., *Naming the Violence,* 1986

Lesbians who are being battered often end up justifying to others their batterers' conduct towards them. The terrible messages that the batterer tells the victim (such as that she is ugly or is nothing without her lover) become internalized to such an extent that the battered lesbian totally believes them about herself.

> Lee Evans and Shelley Bannister, in *Lesbian Ethics,* Spring 1990

There is virtually no literature discussing possible etiologies of battering in lesbian relationships. This can be traced, in part, to denial in the lesbian community about the existence of battering at all.

> Rochelle L. Klinger, in Charles Silverstein, ed., *Gays, Lesbians, and Their Therapists,* 1991

The trade press especially expects queers to be clever and witty, or they want freak stories. The queer press wants the clean sex stories, stories that prove we're the same as heterosexuals, they deny there's anything complicated or nasty or even dangerous about sex stories that say sex is always healthy. In fact, sex is where we act out destructive impulses. There are lots of lesbians in battering relationships, there are lots of obsessive relationships.

> Dorothy Allison, in *Southern Voice* (Atlanta), quoted in *TWN,* May 13, 1992

PETS

The tribade, in search of one of her own kind, has a distinctive badge: this is the magnificent, curled, bedizened, trimmed, sometimes beribboned poodle, which accompanies her on her outings, either on foot or by carriage.

> Léo Taxil, on how to recognize a lesbian "in search of a comrade in vice" on the streets of Paris, *La Corruption fin-de-siècle,* 1891

A woman who loathes the sight of men and dogs, and hates them both cordially, is Miss Augusta Main, a spinster farmer near Berlin, N.Y ... Only in harvest time does she seek outside help, and then she hires strapping young women.

> "She Dislikes Men and Dogs," in the *East Hampton Star,* December 31, 1897

"Here, Sappho Wild Lesbian."

> Emily George, Carrol calling a small tan puppy, *Sappho's Wild Lesbians,* 1984

While some say that lesbian relationships don't have staying power, I totally disagree. I have seen what women have endured from their lover's pets and it's a tribute to enduring affection.

> Gail Sausser, *Lesbian Etiquette,* 1986

I am not a dog lover. I realize this is an irreverent thing for a dyke to say, but it's true.

> Gail Sausser, *More Lesbian Etiquette,* 1990

Do your lover's cats side with your lover in an argument? How do you feel about this?

> Jennifer Hertz and Martha Ertman, Question #142, *Lesbian Queries,* 1990

Love her – love her cats.

> Rhonda Dicksion, Lesbian Survival Hint #30, *The Lesbian Survival Manual,* 1990

Lesbian owners of boy cats: Break the silence, we are everywhere, we are dykes and our kittys have weenies, and we are not ashamed. Claim your own reality! Join us! FFI 645-MEOW.

> "Classlessfied" ad in *Equal Slime Trash* published by Minneapolis's *Equal Time News,* quoted in *Outlines,* August 1990

Consider two stereotypes: gay men and poodles or other "effeminate" dogs ... young girls and horses (*National Velvet*), an interest that precedes the love of boys. Are lesbians supposedly fond of dogs? What is the lesbian pet of choice? ... The image of the dog persuades us that queer passions, the perversities of women who love women and men who love men, are bred into the blood, and are mute, domestic, and subhuman.

> Wayne Koestenbaum, *The Queen's Throat,* 1993

ODDS & ENDS

Girls who put out are tramps. Girls who don't are ladies. That is, however, a rather archaic usage of the word. Should one of you boys happen upon a girl who doesn't put out, do not jump to the conclusion that you have found a lady. What you have probably found is a lesbian.

> Fran Lebowitz, *Metropolitan Life,* 1974

I remember standing on the corner of Portage and Main when I was about sixteen with a sign saying "Gay is Good," and people thought I meant happy and gave me money.

> Robin Tyler, quoted in Val Edwards, in Ed Jackson and Stan Persky, eds., *Flaunting It!,* 1982

The day the homos disappeared, Nora Lindquist had planned a dinner party. First, the bakery didn't have any spinach quiche. Nor could she get any of that delicious key lime pie she'd hoped to impress everyone with ... Her guests arrived late, and two didn't show at all.

> Robin Hardy, "The Day the Homos Disappeared: A Cautionary Tale," in Ed Jackson and Stan Persky, eds., *Flaunting It!,* 1982

Two dykes went their separate routes:
Said one, "I just *don't* give two hoots.
No common tie linked us
Except cunnilinctus,
And a penchant for Brooks Brothers suits."

> Anonymous, "Twenty-five Limericks," in Stephen Coote, ed., *The Penguin Book of Homosexual Verse,* 1983

Goddess grant me the serenity to accept the lovers I cannot change, courage to change the ones I can, and wisdom to know the difference.

> Karen E. Davis, in "Dyke Humor," in *Lesbian Ethics,* Summer 1989

If cruising were music, then lesbian cruising would be Muzak.

> Liz Tracey, in *OutWeek,* quoted in *Outlines,* October 1989

Many years ago I chased a woman for almost two years, only to discover her tastes were exactly like mine: We were both crazy about girls.

> Groucho Marx, quoted in William Cole and Louis Phillips, eds., *Sex: "The Most Fun You Can Have without Laughing" and Other Quotations,* 1990

Number of towns named Dykes in the U.S.: 2

Quoted in *10 Percent,* Winter 1992

...I've got to a point where I can't be politically correct anymore. There are so many things somewhere to annoy people. The vegetarian lesbian alliance will be angry ... I'll get hate letters from the zucchini front.

Robin Williams, quoted in the *New York Times,* December 24, 1992

The Stonewall Card

Name of the first nationally marketed Visa card for gays and lesbians, 1992

Had he lost the election, she would have moved in with Martina Navratilova.

Bob Grant, of Hillary Rodham Clinton, on *The Bob Grant Show,* WABC New York, February 26, 1993

I know that lesbians don't look up at the ceiling when they're making love, but one day I looked up and saw revealed to me the most beautiful fresco ever seen by women — on my lesbian word of honour. It was perfectly real, this fresco, and at the bottom of it was written: a lesbian who does not reinvent the world is a lesbian in the process of disappearing.

Nicole Brossard, in Judith Barrington, ed., *An Intimate Wilderness,* 1991

INDEX